Paul,
Beware of Shapeshifters
in America.

Werewolves, Dogmen, and Other Shapeshifters Stalking North America

By

D1521722

Pamela K. Kinney

Pamela K. Kinney

DreamPunk Press

Werewolves, Dogmen, and Other Shapeshifters Stalking North America

Published by DreamPunk Press, Norfolk, VA
www.dreampunkpress.com
dreamer-in-chief@dreampunkpress.com

Cover art: ©Mohamed Hassan via Pixabay
Cover design by: Tara Moeller
OpenDyslexic font from www.opendyslexic.org

First Edition

ISBN 13: 978-1-954214-08-8 (OpenDyslexic)
ISBN 13: 978-1-954214-07-1 (Deja Vu)
ISBN 13: 978-1-954214-09-5 (e-book)

Printed in the USA

Dedication

This book is dedicated to all those who believe in werewolves, Dogmen, and other kinds of shapeshifters, that they exist outside the pages of fiction, off the movie screens, stalking outside of television shows, and most of all, snarling from all the legends man has ever told since the caveman days. I also dedicate this to my readers: remember, whether by full moon, magic, possession, or maybe even from possible dimensional portals, these shapeshifters and cryptids are stalking the United States of America for you.

Kinney

ACKNOWLEDGMENTS

My first thanks go to my publisher, Dreampunk Press, for publishing this book. I also like to thank my editor, Tara Moeller, for making this book the best it can be.

I also like to thank my husband, Bill, for once more being patient as the dishes and housework fell to the wayside as I read and researched online for my book, then wrote it and edited it. I love you, Bill, because you're one in a million, backing me in all my writing endeavors.

Thanks to all the writers, researchers, and fans of cryptids and werewolves—you made this book possible. Keep on investigating them. As X-Files says: the truth is out there!

Most of all, I like to thank my readers. Without you, there wouldn't be this book or the others I have written and gotten published in the past. No author is an island without their readers. This book acknowledges you, too.

Kinney

CONTENTS

*There is a beast in man that should be exercised,
not exorcised.*
~Anton Lavey

Introduction

Timber wolf at Richmond Metro Zoo in Mosley, Virginia.

Shapeshifters Among Us

It seems that werewolves, dogmen, and other kinds of shapeshifting beings are stalking North America. When one thinks of werewolves, they think of Lon Chaney Jr.'s wolfman, who was bitten by a gypsy werewolf and cursed to change at the full moon every month. As we all know, it was someone who loved him who caused his downfall and ultimate death. Ever since, Hollywood (and yes, even before *The Wolf Man*, there was *Werewolf of London*, released in 1935*)* has been making movies about werewolves—and other shapeshifting beings, too.

Before that, we had writers writing stories about someone becoming a wolf or some other beast. It is still happening. Even before we heard the term Dogman, Whitley Strieber had written a horror novel, *Wolfen*. Wolfen were a race of canine-like creatures living among mankind since man walked the Earth, preying upon us. They resembled the supernatural werewolves, but they didn't turn at the full moon or any other time, either, but were in this shape since birth, mating and birthing young ones and living in packs. They looked like descriptions of the Dogman, way before Linda Godfrey coined the title. These intelligent beasts kept to the country and woods, in the shadows, hunting all types of prey, but man most of all. With humans building villages, towns, and, eventually, cities, they soon stalked their prey among the homeless, who wouldn't be missed. But in the novel, in New York City, those missing were noticed, and the police became involved. A movie based on it was filmed, although they made the creatures look like werewolves that were Native Americans. It was an okay movie, but it was not the book, except for still being set in New York City and the two lead characters. Later, Strieber wrote an actual werewolf horror novel, *The Wild*.

What is a Dogman? Dogman describes a group of more than one type of large cryptozoological beings sometimes described as looking like upright canids. One type of Dogman is said to look like an upright canine, while some witnesses have described what they saw as looking like a Sasquatch with a muzzle instead of having a flat face. Eyewitnesses who have had encounters with the second type mention their beasts as having claws on their fingers and toes' tips, instead of fingernails and toenails, the way a Sasquatch would. Eyewitnesses who have had Dogman encounters often report that they saw the one moving on both on all fours and upright.

Interestingly, whether with a short snout or a longer one, this cryptid looks remarkably like what we thought of as a werewolf for centuries. If these creatures are real, have people seen them in the past, all over the world, and assumed a shapeshifter? Or could this be an actual shapeshifter, captured or killed to prove to others, and it becomes human once more, leaving no evidence of a furry beast? Or did it come from another dimension by a portal to our world, as theories out there mention? It might've been brought here by aliens, as in the same stories concerning Bigfoot, and even the wendigo posted online or published in books. So many ideas and possibilities. Again, just maybe, until we have one brought for proof and DNA testing by scientists, the cryptid is nothing more than a legend.

The first alleged documented Dogman encounter in the United States happened in Wexford County, Michigan, in 1887. Two lumberjacks reported seeing a black, furry creature they described as having a man's body but with a dog's head. Robert Fortney was attacked by five wild dogs in Paris, Michigan, in 1937, and said that one of the five walked on two legs.

The belief in humans that turn into wild predatory animals exists in all major world cultures. And has done so for an exceptionally long time, maybe as far back as prehistoric man. After all, man and woman changed, some shapes never staying, others becoming the next form in evolution, until one day they became the modern humans. So, werewolves are just one way to shift into the shape of an animal. Modern science believes that the stories may have come about as a result of the physical or mental characteristics of humans under the influence of real-life illnesses that made them look or act like wolves.

Reports of dogmen or wolfmen go back to ancient times. One monstrous cannibalistic race that breathed fire and was feared was called the Cynocephali, or Dog-heads. Court physician to Artaxerxes of Persia, Ctesias of Cnidus, wrote of a race of dog-headed men that lived in India in the 4th century BC. Pliny the Elder quoted Ctesias in the 1st century of his work Historia Naturalis. Ctesias said that the Indians of India called the dog-headed men Calystrians, which meant dog-headed in their language, and these beings lived on raw meat.

Of course, some pointed out that Ctesias never went to India and only got all this as hearsay. And that these dogmen might only be monkeys or a race of hairy pygmies called Veddud from Ceylon.

In lore from Egyptians, Queen Hatshepsut sent sailing men to the "Island of Punt" (part of Somalia), and they found dog-headed male warriors there.

For the supernatural version, there are several ways to make the change, according to the myths. One is, of course, the full moon. Another way is by being cursed or bitten—like those criminals cursed by priests who then became werewolves. Though the bitten part is exceedingly rare in lore, unlike how we find it in movies or fiction books. A third way (and I read a book that had something found on a medieval manuscript) is by taking a belt made of wolf fur and chanting some words during the full moon to shift into the wolf form. Another way said they were possessed by demons. Some lycanthropes (according to tales from the 17th century) assured people that they really were wolves and that their fur grew inside their body. Also, to drink rainwater of the paw print of a wolf or drink from enchanted streams also affected metamorphosis.

Werewolves or lycanthropy can be traced back to King Lycaeon of Arcadia's Greek myth, where he was turned into a bloodthirsty wolf by a wrathful Zeus. The story goes that the monarch sacrificed a human child and had the meat cooked and served to the god. The god realized what the meat was and, in vengeful anger, cursed the king.

There is a tale of a baroness who drank from a spring in Germany that caused her to become a werewolf and that her husband, when hunting one night, cut off her paw and later found his wife back in their home, her hand missing. This is the same spring that legend says Hitler urged his "little werewolves", or Gestapo, to drink from.

In Italy, France, and Germany, it was said that a man could turn into a werewolf if he, on a certain Wednesday or Friday, slept outside on a summer night with the full moon shining directly on his face. In other cultures, individuals born during a new moon or suffering from epilepsy, were considered likely to be werewolves.

Ireland has lore about werewolves, like the one concerning St. Patrick. It seems the saint did more than chase snakes from the old sod. He also laid a werewolf curse on a noble Irish family for mocking him.

Lycanthropy is often confused with transmigration; but the essential feature of the were-animal is that it is the alternative form or the double of a living human being, while the soul-animal is the vehicle, temporary or permanent, of the spirit of a dead human being. Still, humans reborn as wolves are often classed with lycanthropy, as well as those instances labelled in local folklore.

There are also tales of humans descending from animals. This is common reasons for tribal and clan origins. One story has the animal assuming human shape, so their human descendants retained their human shapes, while another one has a human marrying a normal animal. North American indigenous traditions mingle the idea of bear ancestors and ursine shifters. Bears would shed their skin and mate with human women in this guise. The resulting offspring might be monsters and yet again, may be born as beautiful children with uncanny strength, even becoming shapeshifters.

One being, Pan Hu from various Chinese legends, is depicted as a supernatural dog, or a canine shapeshifter. Supposedly, he married an emperor's daughter and founded at least one race. He can become human in shape in all parts of him, except for his head. The Chinese stories write that the race descended from him are monsters with combined human and canine anatomy.

The shamanic Turkic peoples believed they are descendants of wolves. They tell a Turkic myth about Asena. Asena is the name of a she-wolf associated with the Oghuz Turkic foundation myth. The legend of Asena tells of a young boy who survived a battle; a female wolf finds the injured child and nurses him back to health. The she-wolf, impregnated by the boy, escapes her enemies by crossing the Western

Sea to a cave near the Qocho mountains and a city of the Tocharians, giving birth to ten half-wolf, half-human boys. Of these, Ashina becomes their leader and establishes the Ashina clan, which ruled over the Göktürk and other Turkic nomadic empires. The first Turks became known as experts in ironworking, as Scythians are also known to have been.

This story of a she-wolf and human boys is similar to the story of the she-wolf who suckled the twins, Romulus and Remus, whose story of one brother killing the other tells the events that led to the founding of the city of Rome and the Roman Kingdom by Romulus. Although the tale takes place before the founding of Rome around 750 BC, the earliest known written account of the myth is from the late 3rd century BC. Possible historical basis for the story, as well as whether the twins' myth was an original part of Roman myth or a later development, is a subject of ongoing debate.

According to the tale, Romulus and Remus were born in Alba Longa, one of the ancient Latin cities near the future site of Rome. Their mother, Rhea Silvia was a vestal virgin and the daughter of the former king, Numitor, who had been displaced by his brother Amulius. In some sources, Rhea Silvia conceived the twins when their father, the god Mars, visited her in a sacred grove dedicated to him.

Seeing them as a possible threat to his rule, King Amulius ordered them to be killed and they were abandoned on the bank of the river Tiber to die. They were saved by the god Tiberinus, Father of the River, and survived with the care of others at the site of what would eventually become Rome. In the well-known myth, the twins were found and suckled by a she-wolf, in a cave now known as the Lupercal. Eventually, they were adopted by Faustulus, a shepherd. They grew up tending flocks, unaware of their true identities. Over time, they became natural leaders and attracted a company of supporters from the community.

There are dog-headed men mentioned in Christian writings, like the Theodore Psalter, which illustrated Jesus Christ preaching to dog-headed men. Others claimed that St. Christopher was a dog-head and that he ate human flesh. They reported him to be enormous, with the head of a dog, a characteristic of the Marmaritae. Speculation said that this Byzantine depiction of St. Christopher as dog-headed might have resulted from a misreading of the Latin term Cananeus (Canaanite) as caninus, that is, "canine".

There are tales of dogmen attacking homes, people, and animals, scaring some people to death, and leaving teeth marks grooving doors' wood. Some fishermen in a boat had to fight off a creature with a man's body but the head of a dog. The monster swam up to their boat through the waters of Claybank Lake in Manistee.

In the Middle Ages of Europe, not only were those accused of being witches prosecuted and burned at the stake, but those accused of being werewolves were done the same. It was thought that lycanthropy was practiced by witches, too. The stories were told that the witches morphed into wolves and roamed the countryside to frighten people, killing and devouring them, too, besides livestock of the humans. Lycanthropes were even believed to be minor demons, and some, whose killer instincts were considered exceptionally strong, were thought to be the Devil himself. Even if the werewolf was not a morphed witch, it was still related to witchcraft: tales were told about witches who arrived at Sabbats mounting these creatures. The evil and wicked acquired, according to Paracelsus (a 16th century alchemist), the shape of a wolf upon death, or could become such creatures if they were cursed by a priest, remaining morphed for seven years.

Although there was the belief that one became a werewolf through a contract with the Devil, others were not so demonic. Those born during the new moon in Italian folk tales would become a werewolf. Anyone who slept under the full moon outside on a Friday would become a werewolf in the same Italian folklore. In the Balkans, they believed that a specific nameless flower (no, not wolfsbane!) turned anyone into a werewolf if they ate it. If someone drank water from a wolf's paw print, or drank from a stream a wolf pack drank at, or ate a wolf's brains, guess what? Yes, these are all ways to become a werewolf. This last belief might connect to rabies, which might include that a bite from a werewolf made you one, except that is a more modern trope thanks to the movie, *The Wolfman*.

If one strips naked, slabs on an ointment, and puts on a wolf skin belt or the whole hide, then say the correct incantations, they can shift. Some legends say to strip naked and roll in the dirt, while others tell you to strip and urinate in a circle drawn on the ground. Some say you have to reverse the ritual to change back to human form, while others mention you becoming human at the end of the night.

In stories that people can shapeshift into various animals, including werewolves and weredogs, this is called "cyanthropy." It comes from cyanthrope—meaning man-dog.

Shamans used magic so they could become animals and birds, or hybrids of man and beast. In parts of the world where there are no wolves, it would be foxes, coyotes, jackals, hyenas, lions, leopards, bears, deer, elk, mountain lion, or dog or cat. Anthropologists believe that shamans inducted young hunters to imagine themselves the predator to hunt and kill their prey. But as we evolved and developed cities, villages, and such, men still feared those, or revered some, who were able to become an animal.

There is even a tale of Sigmund and Sinfjotli, who came across a cabin in the woods owned by victims of a curse, and they found cloaks made of wolf fur and skin. The two slipped the cloaks over their shoulders and became wolves, staying that way for 10 days like the cursed inhabitants of the building did. Once the 10 days ended, they reverted to their human selves and burned the cloaks, ending the curse for good.

I also know that Scandinavians believed that warriors called berserkers could shift into bears and wolves in the heat of battle. These warriors slavered and foamed at the mouth like wolves or growled like bears.

There are more sophisticated ways of assuming an animal shape, by wizards, sorcerers, or shamans projecting their soul into an animal's body. Would this be a true shapeshifting, or using the creature's eyes to see and control its mind?

In Africa, tribes believed that departed chieftains' souls would enter lions' bodies and roam the veldt during the night.

So could sorcerers and warlocks, called nahuals, from an Aztec word, "nahualli." According to lore, the sorcerer uses black magic to change, usually by going into a trance or deep sleep and becoming an animal. Other ways are jumping over a wooden cross and using herbs and ointments containing hallucinogenic ingredients. Some sorcerers could shapeshift at will. In the Southwestern United States, these nahuals are called skinwalkers.

Once they transformed, nahuals could destroy property and perform evil upon people. They would steal and eat livestock and crops, and attack humans. Plus, they would be able to fight other nahuals. Like the European werewolf, they would be wounded in the same spot when they return to human form where someone struck them.

A nahual can be destroyed by stoning, shooting, hanging, and dousing with holy water. The Spaniards introduced the last item from Christian beliefs and practices after their conquest.

Then, there is the lycanthropy used by psychiatrists as a medical word for a disorder in which one *thinks* they can transform into a wolf and then *acts* like one. This term is linked to schizophrenia, multiple personality disorder, bipolar disorder, drug abuse, clinical vampirism, mental retardation, necrophilia, and other psychological disorders.

Features of these "werewolves" include an obsession with the demonic, alienation from self and society, being in cemeteries, and other lonely places. They have a process or ritual of supposed transformation from human to wolf. These people believe they have grown fangs, claws, fur—all the things that would make them a monster. There's an insatiable lust for blood, hypersexual activity like bestiality, and wolfish behavior, including howling, growling, running on all fours, attacking people, and biting them. More frightening, some even kill their victims and eat their flesh before they "change" back to human, experiencing disorientation and depression afterward, as well as impaired mental functioning. This disorder has been around since the 2nd century when Greek physician Galen recognized it. He believed it to be a melancholic disease along with delirium. Marcellus of Rome described the symptoms, and another Greek physician, Paul of Aegina, who based his writings on Marcellus's, was the first to link lycanthropy to melancholia.

Back then, they used bloodletting to "cure" people, but no doubt, it most likely made the condition worse.

During the Inquisition, people were accused, and even convicted, of being werewolves as much as witches of being witches. Some believed the demons made them think they turned into wolves. Others thought they could shapeshift. It didn't help when actual man-eating wolves were killing humans back in medieval times, and many believed that these were werewolves. Many of those accused of witchcraft also confessed to lycanthropy. We now know these people had this medical disorder.

After the Inquisition, many believed this was madness and were put into prisons and institutions until the 19th Century. Most of this mental illness disappeared, except one case between the 19th Century and the 1970s, when Carl G. Jung referred to a case in 1928, and it was called zoanthropy (meaning animals in general). I doubt this mental disease, lycanthropy or zoanthropy, has completely vanished. It just became lumped as paranoia or hysteria. Treatments include antidepressants, neuroleptics, and other medications, along with psychotherapy.

As for someone labeled a werewolf due to possession, there was a case involving paranormal investigators Ed and Lorraine Warren. There is a book about that, although I didn't get it to read for this book. You can find it at Amazon and other dealers. It is titled *Werewolf: A True Story of Demonic Possession* by Ed Warren in paperback, and as *Werewolf* by Lorraine Warren, Robert David Chase, and William Ramsey, in Kindle. Get and read it and determine if you think he was demonically possessed or more likely to have a mental illness.

There is hypertrichosis, where children are born covered in facial and body hair. No doubt, this helped spread belief in werewolfism. One Spanish nobleman, Pedro Gonzalez, was born like this, and it made his life hell, so much so he had to leave the Canary Islands for Switzerland in the seventeenth century. The public became aware of this problem when three brothers with this condition in Mexico made the news in 1986.

The werebeast was called werewolf in Germany, loups-garous in French, French-speaking nations, and Louisiana, lob omen in Portugal, lob ombre in Spain, and lupo manaro in Italy. Sadly, fear of the wolf has cause men to exterminate the animals. No longer can we find a wolf (outside of a zoo) in Britain or Germany, and even in the United States except Alaska, although wolves have been reintroduced in some state parks—like timber wolves and red wolves. They thought France might be wolfless, but the discovery of a small pack in 1963 changed that, plus there are wolves seen in Canada, Northern Italy, even Spain, Turkey, Poland, and Portugal.

The werewolf hunt, kill, and eat their prey. They might only go after flocks of sheep or cattle, even wild deer, but some werewolves committed cannibalism, particularly raping a child or young girl, then eating them.

One well-known werewolf who engaged in cannibalism was Peter Stubb, or Stump, in 16th century Germany. He was supposedly given a wolf belt by the Devil to become a werewolf and terrorized the countryside for 25 years. He did kill and eat cattle and sheep, but he killed people a lot more, especially those who may have offended him just one time. He did not eat the male adults he killed, but he raped, killed, and fed on women and young girls. He murdered 13 children and two pregnant women. The monster even killed and ate his son! He had incest with his daughter, who gave birth to his child, and also with his sister. He had many concubines, even one he claimed was a succubus sent by the Devil.

Supposedly pursued in his wolf form, Stubb tried getting away by taking off his wolf belt and becoming a man again. It didn't work, as his pursuers captured him and brought him before a magistrate. Found guilty and tortured, the town of Bedburg executed him. They placed his head on a pole outside of town as a warning to all. No need for silver bullets or swords, or anything else used against werewolves; Stubb died.

As for werewolves not in league with the Devil, people killed those in the usual way, like ordinary murderers, with clubs, knives, and guns. Once wounded or dead, the wolf supposedly reverted to its human shape.

A story from 16th-century France told of a hunter who fought off a wolf and cut off its front paw before it ran off. He stuck it in his pouch and went home. Before he arrived there, he ran into a friend and told him his tale, then reached into the bag to retrieve the paw. He pulled out a woman's hand with a gold ring on the wedding finger. The hunter recognized the ring and ran home, where he found his wife bandaging her stump. Local officials tried his wife, and they burned her at the stake.

There are many ways to keep a werewolf away from you and your home. In Britain, rye, mistletoe, ash, and yew trees keep the beast away. There is the story that werewolves fear running water (like vampires won't cross water), so wading across a creek or a river might save a person's life.

One can tell who a werewolf is, too. The telltale ways are straight, slanting eyebrows meeting over the nose, reddish fingernails that are long and curving, small ears set back in the head, a long third finger on each hand, and extreme amounts of hair, especially on their hands and feet. Sometimes there is no way to tell a werewolf in their human form, although they are bigger, fiercer, and hungrier than the regular human. Not all werewolves look alike, as some folklores say some have a wolf's head on a human body while others might look like a wolf with human hands.

Some thought, going back to prehistoric times when shamans or priests wore animal masks—and even hunters did, too—helped the hunter capture and kill their prey. But another idea for werewolves, even dogmen, could be traced back to ancient Egypt and Anubis. The lower body of this Egyptian god is human, but the head is that of a jackal. Other gods had animal heads, like Bastet, Horus, Sekmet, Ra, Heket, Tefnut, Amun, Geb, Hathor, Sobek, and Thoth.

Arlene Wolinski, an archaeologist, wrote an article that appeared in the American periodical, *Archaeology*, "Egyptian Masks: The Priest and His Role." In this article, Wolinski explains that paintings we see are not the gods but the priests wearing the god's mask in a ceremony. Had outsiders seen these priests and thought "shapeshifters"? Not that it covers all the shapeshifter folklore; still, it's an exciting premise. There were possibly even cults involved with Anubis, where men wore dog heads or masks in Rome. There was a statue of a man in a Roman tunic with a dog's head, titled "Hermanubis," pointed out by Wolinski. The name Hermanubis comes from the Roman god, Mercury, joined with Anubis. And when Germanic peoples were recruited by Romans in their armies, of course, they would have seen these priests with the dog-head masks and carried tales of man-wolves or man-dogs back to their homelands.

Nowadays, it appears werewolves, dogmen, and other kinds of shapeshifting beings have always been stalking in America and all over the world, and not just by our legends and myths, but by authors writing fictional tales and books. When many think of werewolves, they think of Lon Chaney Jr.'s movie wolf man, who was bitten by a gypsy werewolf and cursed to change at the full moon every month. As we all know, it was someone who loved him that caused his downfall and ultimate death. Ever since, Hollywood (and yes, even before *The Wolf Man*, there was the 1913 movie, *The Werewolf*), werewolves of all kinds graced the silver screen and the small screens of our televisions. Not just wolfmen, but other beasts that humans can metamorphosis into, like cats in both the 1942 and 1982 versions of *Cat*

People. Actually, more like black wereleopards or werepanthers. Both films were well done and frightening, eerie, even erotic. There are other movies with shifters that do not turn into wolves. Such as *Hyenas* from 2011, and *Junoon* from 1992, in which a man is nearly killed by a cursed tiger and becomes one himself every full moon. Not all become predators, as in one New Zealand movie, *Black Sheep*, a genetic experiment changes sheep on a farm into monstrous killers. You can find this horror flick to watch for free at YouTube. Even video games have shifters in them. It appears we cannot get away from the animal hidden within us.

A note: if werewolves or other shapeshifters did exist, a good time to catch one might have been Saturday night in Halloween 2020. When my husband and I drove to a spot near Chesterfield County Tech Center, I spied the blue moon (meaning this was the second moon that month, not colored blue) as it hung bright and gorgeous, and no, I never encountered a single werewolf that night. At least not at 10 o'clock that night. The only werewolf was in the movie I streamed earlier, *The Wolf of Snow Hollow*. But again, we didn't get trick or treaters in our neighborhood and Halloween that night was a quiet one. It appeared that even werewolves were afraid of what 2020 and Covid might do to them, even on a Halloween full-moon night that hadn't been seen since the 1940s. Virus trumped werewolf—who knew?

Anyway, turn the page and you will find plenty of werewolves, dogmen, ottermen, skinwalkers, and all sorts of shapeshifters and those who might be mistaken for shifters stalking North America. And sometimes, not all are ruled by the full moon. Just be sure to have silver bullets on hand.

Just in case.

WEREWOLVES

"The story goes that he who tastes of the one bit of human entrails minced up with those of other victims is inevitably transformed into a wolf."
~Plato

Werewolves in Virginia

Hunger drives the wolf out of the wood.

~English Proverb

Werewolf (Public Domain)

Werewolf of Henrico (Henrico County)

Werewolves, also known as lycanthropes, are mythological humans who can change their shapes into that of wolves or wolf-like creatures. This either occurs by being bitten by another werewolf (this comes from the movies) or placed under a curse. According to medieval lore, one can take a belt made of wolf fur and, by wearing only it and nothing else while chanting during the full moon, be able to shift that way.

Did the "Werewolf of Henrico" use one of these methods? Or is it nothing more than misidentification of a couple of dogs? I couldn't find proof of its existence when I first heard about it and investigated the story for my ghost book, *Haunted Virginia: Legends, Myths, and True Tales*. The monster has been mostly seen in the Highland Springs area, hanging around the Confederate Hills Recreation Center (now renamed to Springs Recreation Center) and the Osborn Boat Landing. Whatever the case, I think it is cool that Richmond can now not only brag about a resident vampire but a werewolf, too. Neither has ever faced off like vampires and werewolves in the movies and fiction, at least not that I've heard.

Described as having a human's body and an animal's face, it runs on all fours or on its hind legs. It stands at 6 feet tall, is covered in gray or white hair, and has only been seen under the full moon; it is harmless, except for charging at people. Of course, experts in the paranormal say it is most likely a Bigfoot. Still, the full moon angle smacks of a werewolf.

Another person who saw it posted his experience on a "werewolf" website. The man said that he and a girlfriend enjoyed the full moon at Osborn Boat Landing, near the river, and were talking when they heard some eerie howls. The noise shocked the young woman, and when the young man turned, he saw two massive, stocky-built white dogs in the light. The animals lingered for what had to be about 10 minutes. Unable to run to their vehicle parked a hundred yards away, the man and his girlfriend froze. One of the creatures walked over to the pavilion not far from where they stood, leaped onto the picnic table for a few seconds, then jumped off, ran over to his car, and checked it out. It took its time as it made its way over to the trees, while the other one remained in the shadows.

Lucky for the pair, their rescue came as another car drove up. First, one of the creatures howled at the other vehicle, and then they crashed back into the trees. Both the guy and his girlfriend took their chance for escape, hoping the other one wouldn't chase them, and bolted to his car and jumped in. The young man drove onto the road and paused by the wooded area the animals escaped into and, using a flashlight, stabbed the trees with the light, but he didn't see any sign of the beasts. The couple vowed never to go back there after dark ever again.

A man used to live with his parents on Old Osborne Turnpike, and their house is right next to the Battlefield Park. They have a large, unfenced backyard, with a field going back about a hundred yards into the woods, which continue into the park. When he and his wife had started dating, she would visit him and stay over some nights. Both would go behind his house and sit on a picnic table to smoke because they couldn't smoke in the house.

During some of these nights, when it was late (about 2 or 3 in the morning), they would hear awful howling noises. It often creeped them out so much they put out the cigarettes and rushed back into the house.

One time during the day, they went outside to smoke and sat on the picnic table. They saw a pack of white canines heading toward them, not running but slowly making their way across the neighbors' backyards. The dogs came into his backyard and walked across the yard, right in front of them. The animals walked right across the yard, across the field, making for a neighbor's yard on the other side. Had they seen the werewolf of Henrico, maybe a pack of them, or just dogs?

Another experience happened 9 years ago. The man's family owned a pet cat that they always let outside. It was his father's birthday, and they had let the cat outside for a while as they sat around the table, eating birthday cake. Suddenly, something crashed into the glass back door, and everyone ran out to see what it was. They found the cat lying on the ground, covered in animal feces. The cat remains indoors now, refusing to go out. Was this done by the werewolf of Henrico, or something else?

Richmond has its vampire, and now it has its werewolf, but don't look anytime soon for them facing off like in the movies. It seems that the werewolf stalks the woods of Henrico County. The next time you stop for the night at Osborn Boat Landing, make sure you have silver bullets in a pistol on you.

Confederate Hills Recreation Center, now Springs
Recreation Center

Werewolf Sighting in Prince William
(Prince William)

Someone in a Woolridge neighborhood was
walking at around at 10 at night when they saw
what they thought at first was a dog in the
woods near a shopping center, but then peering
at it, they thought it looked more wolf- or
coyote-like. It rose onto its hind legs, and
frightened, the person made a 911 call to the
Prince William County Police. They dispatched
a patrol car to the neighborhood, but the officer
didn't find hide nor hair of the "werewolf," as
the police spokesman for the police department
told InsideNoVa.com. Maybe the beast had
shifted to its human form by then?

An 8-year-old boy was sleeping in his bed
when something awoke him. The sound came
from his bedroom window, and he looked up.

He saw the face of a monster, human-like but with a snout of a dog and yellow eyes! The thing was looking through the glass at him! Frightened, the boy ran from the room to his mother. Of course, she assumed he'd had a nightmare, but she let him sleep in her room. The boy never saw the monster again.

Werewolf of Big Stone Gap (Big Stone Gap)

Some years after the Civil War ended, a legend arose of a werewolf seen in the mountain forests of the Appalachian Mountains in the southwestern tip of Virginia. Accused of killing sheep and other farm animals, it was even blamed for several young women's mysterious disappearances in the area. This beast so frightened the locals that they refuse to venture outdoors when the full moon moved across the night sky.

A hunter was out hunting when he saw it. Thinking it was an escaped circus animal or a mountain lion, he tried to track it, but it eluded him. Months later, as he slept on a rocky ledge, he woke up and found the creature staring at him. It was the largest and strangest wolf he had ever seen.

He fired his rifle at it, but the creature got away into some brush. He returned a week later with some bloodhounds to track it but didn't find any tracks, just a small amount of dried blood. He took a sample to be analyzed. The answer that came back was that it was human blood.

Whether wolf or human, the werewolf was never seen again.

Dismal Swamp Dogman/Werewolf— Suffolk, Virginia

The werewolf stalked the Dismal Swamp area of the Suffolk, Virginia side in the late 1800s to the early 1900s.

An 8-year-old boy who lived on the edge of the Great Dismal Swamp on the Virginia side was in bed one night. The sky was cloudless, or just very bright (he never thought until recently as an adult whether the moon was shining or not) and saw a beast looking right through his window at him. He could see drool running from its fangs, and its eyes were looking straight at him. It was supposedly standing on its hind legs and had cream, red, and brown-colored, matted fur, and a face almost like a wolf's. Other than its snout, its facial features were very human, with high jawbones. The area around its eyes and its eyes, too, appeared humanlike He thought the eyes were yellow.

The boy crawled out of bed and ran straight to his mother's room, where she let him stay the night. In the morning, they looked around outside, and they found grass yanked out beneath his bedroom window, but no discernable footprints there or elsewhere in the yard. There were actual scratches in the wood under his window, and paint was missing, too.

Another encounter with the Dismal Swamp werewolf was by Edward Smith. One night, he heard his dogs making a racket and thinking that it might be a fox getting into his chickens, he grabbed his shotgun and stepped outside. Suddenly, one of his dogs gave a loud screech. Worried that maybe it was something worse than a fox, he rushed into the yard. The moon lit enough of the area, and he saw not a fox, but something else standing over one of his hounds. It stood on its hind legs, much taller than his own 6-foot height. It had to be a bear, most likely rearing up onto its back legs. It turned its head, and the moonlight revealed not a bear's face, but what looked like a wolf, with sharp, pointed ears, glowing yellow eyes, and a short snout that it had opened, moonlight glinting on sharp fangs. It stood easily on its hind feet, as if that was natural to it.

Frightened, Smith shot at the beast, twice. It whipped around and ran away on its hind legs like a man would, vanishing into the shadowy trees toward where the Dismal Swamp would be. Smith ran over to his dog and found it hurt, but not dead. The only blood he found came from his dog, but nothing to show him if he'd hit the creature.

Whatever the wolf-thing was, he never had problems with it again.

Another time, someone had an encounter with the bipedal wolfman, it was a little girl who was asleep in her bedroom when she heard sounds at the window. She looked up and saw a horrific face looking in at her. She screamed, and her parents rushed in seconds later. When she told her parents about her visitor, pointing at her window, they didn't see anything. She told her parents that it looked like a big dog or wolf. Her father grabbed his hunting gun and ran outdoors to search but found nothing. The next morning, he did find large footprints in the dirt just under her window. The thing was, the window was about 6 feet from the ground and if a dog or wolf was looking in by rearing up on its rear legs, it had to be a very big animal.

There were a few more incidents concerning the 'werewolf', as people began calling it; even hunters began hunting for it. One man, Harrison Walker, claimed to have killed it, but he never showed a carcass, and sightings continued through to the early 1900s, until they stopped. Was it a shapeshifter, a Dogman, or even a sasquatch?

White Wolf
West Virginia, When Still Part of Virginia

When West Virginia was still a part of Virginia, timberwolves roamed the area and killed local farms' livestock. Mountain man Bill Williams had earned himself a reputation as a wolf killer. He earned ten dollars for each wolf he killed, and he brought at least five hundred a year for 5 years. Since he made enough money to do so, he retired.

But he came out of retirement when a white wolf appeared, attacking and killing cattle. He tried to shoot it, even trap it, but it proved futile. No one ever caught it, and not one bullet appeared to stroke its flesh. There were rumors spread across the land that it was a werewolf. The people asked for Williams' help, but he refused.

But when Williams found one of his cows half-eaten, he became enraged. He grabbed his rifle and tracked the beast. When he felt sure of its lair, he tied a lamb to a tree, hid nearby, and waited in the night.

When Williams didn't return the next day, his neighbors went searching for him. They found the lamb, still tied to the tree and alive. They found Williams—his throat torn out, his eyes wide with horror, but most odd, they couldn't find any sign of tracks or sign of a struggle.

Ghost or werewolf, no one could say, but no one saw the white wolf ever again.

Encounter in the Eighties
Southwestern Virginia

Early in the 1980s, a man was driving through a wooded area of the southwestern part of Virginia. He didn't pass any other vehicle and it was quiet, when suddenly, he spied a large shadow detach from the trees on one side of the road. To his shock, he saw what looked like a wolf or dog on its hind legs, running like a human being would. It ran to the side of his car and frightened, he revved up his engine and raced away. The creature gave chase. He couldn't believe that it kept pace with his car. Finally, it gave up and retreated away from the road and back into the trees.

Wolf Girl
Western Virginia

The following true tale came from a pamphlet on western Virginia folklore on file at the Library of Congress in Washington D.C., as told to Robert Swick by his grandfather as truth.

It seems that a family traveling westward died of some disease in the mountains, maybe from malaria, the only survivors being twin baby girls. A female wolf who'd lost her pups took both babies to her den to care for them.

Robert Swick's grandfather's relative was hunting with others when they all heard a whining. They searched for what made the noise and came upon the wolf in her den, nursing two naked baby girls. The she-wolf bolted in fear, but the toddlers rose on all fours and growled at the men. The men managed to pick them up and take them home.

The girls appeared to be 2 years old. They only ate raw meat. The one twin they named

Anna died of pneumonia. The other, Annette, grieved for the loss of her sister.

It took some time, but they got her to learn to use utensils, sit and stand upright, and begin to use human speech. By the time Annette was 16, she had appeared like any normal human girl of the times, although she did retain some animal instincts.

Two years later, she became engaged to a ministerial student. A month before her wedding, she went walking with her fiancée in the woods when they came upon a pack of wolves in a clearing. One of the wolves howled, and her young man picked up a limb for protection, but Annette dropped to all fours and trotted over to the canines. Her fiancée said it was like they had a reunion.

He yelled, but she ignored him, and when the wolves loped off, she went with them. The man and others organized a search party and went looking for Annette, but they never found her.

Werewolves of West Virginia

I think we all have to fight the werewolf within us somehow.
~William Kempe, Actor

When West Virginia separated officially from Virginia and it became the 35th state on June 20, 1863, it didn't leave its werewolves and other monsters behind in the Old Dominion. It was formed because of the Civil War. Same as the North battled South in the country, the western part of what was then still Virginia confronted the eastern part of Virginia. After all, they may have formed a single state in name, but not in geography, economy, climate, or the descent of its residents or way of life. It was originally part of the British Virginia Colony (1607–1776) and the western part of the state of Virginia (1776–1863).

They refused to secede from the Union when Virginia decided to, and thought it was treasonous. They stood for the Union and declared themselves independent. Western Virginia was settled largely by Germans and Scotch-Irish, and the mountains isolated them besides making them independent. Their communities differed sharply from the eastern part of Virginia, with its population mostly of English descent. Thoughts of their own secession began as early as 1829. In fact, they even had a name for it. There was a convention of delegates from western Virginia who met in Wheeling in 1861, for the purpose of forming the "State of Kanawha," which incorporated 39 counties. The name honored a Native American tribe and a major state river, which was also called Kanawha. When the constitution for the proposed state was finalized in 1862, the name had changed to the more generic West Virginia.

Now, the U.S. Constitution doesn't allow a new state to be formed, not without the consent of the original state. With Virginia having left the Union, Western Virginia delegates formed a reorganized government of Virginia, then that government granted itself permission to form the state of West Virginia. President Abraham Lincoln reluctantly approved statehood. For West Virginia had seceded from Virginia, who seceded from the U.S., and West Virginia's was a secession in favor of the Union, so it was tolerated.

The westerners were divided. Few slaves were in the lands held by western farmers, who resented the political power of eastern slave owners. And yet, pro-Confederate majorities existed in 24 of the 48 counties, and Confederate sympathizers were active in the others, and so, West Virginia provided troops to both the Union and the Confederacy. The state is the birthplace of General Stonewall Jackson, and we all know who he fought for.

The state later became known for labor strife, natural resources, and economic struggles. It also claims to be the birthplace of Mother's Day. Waves of immigrants settled there in the early 1900s. West Virginians became known as hillbillies, too, much to the chagrin of many West Virginians not like that at all. One time, the West Virginia University student paper denounced nationally syndicated radio host Jim Bohannon's observation that there's nothing to do in Morgantown but "mine coal and molest livestock."

So, what has all this history of the state have to do with Mothman, werewolves, Wampus cat, the Snallygaster, Bigfoot, sheepsquatch, black dogs, ghosts, and all the other monsters and legends? Most likely, nothing, and yet, history can define why a ghost may be haunting a house or a werewolf lurking in the area. Maybe again, shifters and all those other beasties may just be in the area, due to the mountainous ranges and woods, and then, there is that United States national radio quiet zone in the state: A large area of land in the United States designated as a radio quiet zone, in which radio transmissions are heavily restricted by law to facilitate scientific research and the gathering of military intelligence. Roughly half of the zone is located in the Blue Ridge Mountains of west-central Virginia while the other half is the Allegheny Mountains of east-central West Virginia; a small part of the zone is in the southernmost tip of the Maryland panhandle. Although not all are not permitted, emergency service (police, fire, and ambulance) radios and CB radios are allowed. What has this to do with werewolves, dogmen, or anything else? Probably nothing, but again, maybe in an area like this, werewolves don't have to worry about someone sighting them and taking a photo with their phone or calling 911.

There has been a reality TV show called *Mountain Monsters*, shown on *Travel Channel* There was the 10th episode of season 1, titled "Werewolf of Webster County," from a few years ago. Now, I really didn't believe some of the stuff on the show—it reminded me too much of fiction novels and the guys acting too much like the kind of West Virginians the state rather be forgotten. But there are many encounters mentioned in books and on websites that sound more realistic. So, I will be sharing those tales in this chapter, and the folklore, too.

The White Wolf of French Creek

This piece of folklore is from Upshur County, in the area of French Creek.

During the mid-1800s, a white creature roamed around the outskirts of French Creek. Townspeople were frightened, as the last wolf sighting had been quite a few years prior to the sighting of this albino animal. One farmer said that the white beast had killed several of his sheep and escaped after being shot three times. Later in the same month, this creature stalked the French Creek area and this time, was shot at close range by hunters. The wolf had succeeded in killing various farm animals and pets while evading death. People were beginning to whisper that the creature was a supernatural entity and feared that a human might fall victim to its gnashing fangs.

Bill Williams was a local in the French Creek area and had been a well-known wolf hunter in earlier years when wolves dominated the countryside. He had killed hundreds of wolves in the past and became wealthy due to the bounties paid upon presentation of a wolf carcass. He had also sworn to never take up a rifle to kill a wolf again, but his view was soon to change.

The wolf's latest kill was one of Bill's cows and Bill set out with his trusted rifle to track the murderous animal and put an end to the town's apprehension. Using a lamb tied to a stake in an area where he figured the wolf would attack, Bill waited in the darkness figuring a quick kill. The next morning, to the horror of local townspeople, Bill Williams, the great wolf hunter, was found dead. The lamb was unharmed, alive, and still tied to the wooden stake. Bill had suffered greatly and lay dead and cold. Apparently, the corpse had been the victim of a grisly death. His neck had been ripped and mostly torn from the stiff body with no traces of blood or paw tracks anywhere.

Many believed the white wolf to be an avenging spirit, because Bill broke a vow not to hunt wolves. Others believed it to be demonic, exacting death at will again and again. Across the state of West Virginia, white wolves continue to be seen and always escape death or capture by simply seeming to disappear into the night air.

Elkins has also had its share of white wolf sightings. These sightings always occur on full moons, just like on television and in folklore. All attempts to catch or kill the white predator has been in vain. The evasive carnivore returns full moon after full moon, filling its stomach with its prey repeatedly.

It's unclear if the white wolf still haunts any human in French Creek after Bill's death, but tales of white wolves still circulate in remote areas of West Virginia.

Blue Devil

For about a year from 1939-1940, some blue, dog-faced creature that resemble a wolf or coyote and about the size of a pony, was the blame for livestock attacks and the death of one hunting dog. It stalked the areas of Grassy Creek and Jumbo, but the thing was, no one ever really saw it.

On December 13, 1939, the *Charleston Daily Mail* reported that it had killed a hound of John Clevenger of Jumbo when the canine began trailing it through some woods. The newspaper also reported that Edgar Cogar of Jumbo also claimed that the same thing harassed his sheep and cattle at night, causing them to mill about in a restless manner. One pf his cows was attacked and wounded by the Blue Devil, too.

There were posses from Buckhannon, Webster, and Charleston that had been formed to pursue the beast, but they never captured anything. Two hunters from the state of New York brought their hunting dogs with them to see if they could capture this elusive animal, but when the dogs caught the sent and took off, they returned whimpering and with their tails between their legs, refusing to follow the scent after that.

By this time, residents considered petitioning the state conservation commission, to either investigate to prove it was real or not, or hunt it. The Blue Devil became not a creature of legend, but something to poke fun at, like the *Charleston Daily Mail* did in stating it was nothing more than a giant mole. Another newspaper, the *Wheeling News-Register*, didn't want anything to do with "strange animals." Yet, something kept killing sheep.

Glen Fisher of Bill Fisher Hollow told the press that he had killed the Blue Devil in 1939, that he shot at a strange animal that his bullet struck and that it leaped into the air. In the morning, he went to search for a carcass, but found nothing, not even blood. But he said that no more of the livestock had been killed since then.

The Blue Devil maybe didn't die or maybe it was another one; either way, it appeared later in the Elk River and Middle Mountain area. A bounty of 200 dollars was put up after a series of sheep and cattle being killed, and even some humans attacked. The bounty amount was matched by the state commission and another 25 dollars was thrown in by the Valley Head Rod and Gun Club. A miner from Weaver, Elmer Corley, called on December 4, 1940 to say he had finally killed the Blue Devil. He said he wasn't sure if what he killed was positively the Blue Devil, but still wanted his reward money. He brought the carcass to the district game protector, C.T. Whittacre, who examined it and said it looked like a coyote, but he couldn't be certain of its identity.

Webster County Werewolf

Years later, another werewolf-type beast was encountered in Webster County. Two men and their sons camped out on Cranberry Ridge, there to do some hunting with other hunters. It had been a warm day in the mountainous area, and a heavy rain arrived by evening. After they discovered they forgot lard for cooking, the two cousins volunteered to ride in by ATV into Nicholas County to pick up that and some other items. Decked out in rain gear due to the rain, they took off through Tunnel Ridge, until they came upon Gauley River.

The rain had stopped, and clouds parted to reveal a full moon. Their ATV got stuck in some mud and they got off to try and get it out. That was when one of the cousins noticed an enormous wolf standing on its hind legs like a man would. It stood on the trail behind them. It appeared to look about 6 feet tall, maybe even taller than that.

The cousin who saw it, thought, *Werewolf!* He told his cousin who had finally gotten the ATV out of the mud, to look back and see what he was seeing.

Both frightened, they jumped onto the ATV and roared away. Neither looked back to even see if the creature pursued them, and just drove to the one cousin's house, stopped the machine, and leaped off, running inside the home.

Scared to go back on their ATV, they begged the cousin's mother to drive them back to the camp. After loading the ATV into the truck's bed, the woman drove them to where her husband and brother-in-law waited. The boys told what had happened, but no one at camp had seen any wolfman and thought it had only been their imagination.

Dogman or Werewolf?

On Sandy Huff Hollow near Iager in McDowell County, there had been a dog-like creature that ran on all fours, but also had been caught running and walking on its hind legs. It was blamed for missing chickens, cat, and dogs, and hunters claimed to have been stalked by it. One woman who lived in a trailer saw it looking in her window one evening. Scared, she shut off all lights in her place, but it still terrorized her all night, by banging on her trailer and scratching the outside wall.

Rougarou (Loup-Garou)
Louisiana

Man is to man either a god or a wolf.
~Desiderius Erasmus

Rougarou (Public Domain)

Loup is French for wolf, and garou (from Frankish garulf, cognate with English werewolf) is a man who transforms into an animal for 101 days. It is also known as the Rougarou and is a monster from Cajun folklore.

In the legend, the description of this beast has a man's body and the head of a wolf or a dog, and it prowls the Louisiana swamps looking for misbehaving children. It sounds not unlike the descriptions of the dogmen from witnesses. The stories of the rougarou were most likely inspired by European stories of werewolves the Cajun people brought with them from Canada as they migrated to

Louisiana. Some people call the monster rougarou; others refer to it as the loup-garou. According to Barry Jean Anklet, an academic expert on Cajun folklore and professor at the University of Louisiana, the tale of the rougarou/loup-garou is a common legend across the state.

How a person transforms into a monster doesn't seem to be entirely clear, though it is a belief to be the fate of those who violate the rules of the Catholic observance of Lent. Nor is it clear if the rougarou only prowls during a full moon, like a werewolf. One thing that seems inevitable is that some of the rougarou's preferred haunts are the swamps of central and eastern Louisiana. Although encounters with the creature have happened in other states and Canada, where the French have settled.

Besides a werewolf, there is a belief a loup-garou can also transform into a cow, horse, or any other animal. It also has mental powers and can control a human victim, making the human become an enraged animal roaming fields and pastures at night. When it becomes daytime, the unfortunate person returns to their human form too sickly and fearful of telling what happened to them.

After that time, stories that have been told by elders to persuade Cajun children to behave relate that the curse is transferred from person to person when the rougarou curses another. According to another variation, the wolf-like beast will hunt down and kill Catholics who do not follow Lent's rules. This last variant coincides with the French Catholic loup-garou stories, according to which the method for turning into a werewolf is to break Lent 7 years in a row.

A standard blood-sucking legend says that the rougarou is under a spell for 101 days. After that time, the curse is transferred from person to person when the rougarou draws another human's blood. During that day, the creature returns to human form. Although acting sickly, the human refrains from telling others of the situation for fear of being killed. Other stories include the cause of the rougarou as due to witchcraft. In the latter claim, only a witch can make a rougarou—either by turning into a wolf herself or cursing others with lycanthropy. Supposedly, there are tales of the loup-garou, or witch wolf, whom no bullet could kill. Another way to free someone of the curse would be when someone cuts a cross into the hand, on the paw, or the nose. As University of

Louisiana doctorate student Rachel Doherty wrote in her dissertation about the creature, as posted at thevermillion.com, in the article, "Werewolves of the Swamp," the loup-garou has terrorized South Louisiana for decades.

She also says that the person is cursed because they did something shameful, usually something that goes against religion. If someone behaves lowly, they are knocked down to a lower state, like a beast.

The creature is featured in an episode of *Cajun Justice*, an *AE* television show. A camp owner alerted authorities and videotaped what he suspected to be a rougarou in the weeds behind his camp. The legend of the rougarou plays a prominent role in the *History Channel* television series *Cryptid: The Swamp Beast*. An unknown creature has been mutilating and killing animals and perhaps humans in southern Louisiana; some locals attribute the attacks to a rougarou. Similarly, in episode 6 of *Swamp Mysteries*, Troy Landry discusses the rougarou legend while hunting a creature, killing Voodoo Bayou's pets.

The Rougarou, or loup-garou, has been a feature in other television shows and movies, too. A rougarou is a monster of the week in Season 4, Episode 4 of *Supernatural*, titled

Metamorphosis. The rougarou was incorporated into the story of an episode of the American television show *NCIS: New Orleans*. In the episode, a victim is killed while investigating a possible sighting of the rougarou, which occurs in the 20th episode of the show's sixth season. The 2015 short crime film *Atchafalaya* centers around a game warden searching in a Louisiana swamp for a missing person hinted to have been taken by a loup-garou. You can watch it at https://vimeo.com/193399387.

Werewolves and Witches

If you live among wolves you have to act like a wolf.
~Nikita Khrushchev

Witches and werewolves have existed together. Not only did they burn witches in Europe, but those accused of being werewolves were arrested and executed. Many people also believed that witches could shapeshift, too.

What about witches here in America? Remember what happened in Puritan-settled Salem, Massachusetts? Of course, we now know many were innocent of the crime there. But historian Chadwick Hansen, using original records, wrote in his 1969-published *Witchcraft of Salem* that though many were not guilty of the crime of witchcraft, there was no doubt a few, plus others in other areas of Massachusetts and elsewhere, actually practiced it. Sadly, there may have been those practicing witchcraft in secret, but innocents (like Grace Sherwood in Pungo, Virginia) were accused, went through a trial, ducked in rivers, and put in prison, or in the case of Salem, hung until they were dead. In Grace's case, they imprisoned her for 7 years and 10 months. Released in 1714, Grace paid the back taxes on her property and returned to her farm, where she worked the land until her death at 80 years of age in September 1740.

One of the things witches could do was transform into something else. Like in tall tales told later, witnesses claimed Grace Sherwood could become a firefly, so she could "dance" in the moonlight. At the same time, the Inquisition in Europe accused werewolves of using baby's fat to transform.

Witches and devils have been in Virginia since the first colonists settled in Jamestown. In L. B. Taylor's *Ghosts of Virginia Volume VI*, he mentions King James saying how "devils" were considered to be in wild areas of the world and that the Devil was present in places of greatest ignorance and barbarity. One can imagine what

John Smith and the other settlers thought when they saw the Indigenous natives with their dances, painted faces, and other indigenous traditions.

Virginia seemed a dwelling place of evil and a battleground between the forces of good and evil. Idols worshiped by Indigenous Peoples were considered representations of the Devil. John Smith himself considered one such idol, "Okee," to be a "devil-witch." When one of the colonists, Alexander Whitaker, and others with him, explored the Nansemond River, they came upon some Indigenous Peoples dancing. One of the dancers told them that there would be rain shortly. When a storm struck, Whitaker wrote, "All which things make me think that there be great witches amongst them and they (are) very familiar with the devil."

Unlike the cases in Salem, Massachusetts, where women had been accused unjustly and declared guilty, then hung, Virginia seemed to handle the witchcraft thing much better. To curb runaway charges of witchcraft, like in New England, the Virginia General Assembly passed in 1662, "An Act for Punishment of Scandalous Persons." It stated that women who acted peculiar and scandalous and caused their husbands to bring suits against their wives, accusing them of witchcraft, the woman would be punished by being ducked after the judgment was passed. If the person who accused the other of witchcraft lost in court, the damages were adjusted at a significant amount for the slanderer to pay, along with 500 pounds of tobacco.

This would make anyone think carefully before accusing someone of witchcraft or suing for slander if another accused their wife or husband of being a witch.

Guardian of the Witch Cottage

There are stories that shamans or witches could summon animal spirits to protect the dead, treasure, or even property. Like what happened in Edgerton, Wisconsin, when teenagers living near Lake Koshkonong in the 1970s raided a cottage believed to once have been inhabited by a witch.

Centuries before, Indigenous tribes lived near the lake—believed to have a terrifying water monster in it. The beast would overturn their canoes and drag them down to the depths of the lake, killing them. It always plugged white clay in their nostrils as proof it had done the terrible deed.

Two 15-year-old girls (I will call them Jenny and Carol) lived in year-round residences (there were also vacation places) and heard about several frame cottages near the water that were once lived in by witches. Just like teenagers everywhere, and even today, they decided they would check them out. So, they invited another girl and three boys to join them. Using only flashlights to see their way since they did this after dark, the group headed over to the buildings.

They peeked through windows, and most were empty, but they found one that still had some of its furniture and found it unlocked after testing the door. They stepped inside and looked around in all of the rooms. The floral wallpaper was still on the walls, although a bit yellowed with age. Boxes of old magazines sat in the corner of one room, which still had a brass bed, minus its mattress. The teens thought it would be fun to take some souvenirs of their nighttime trip and began to take the bed apart. One of the girls found a leather-bound book with spells and potions written by hand on its yellowing pages. They snatched that, too.

Suddenly, an old hand-cranked Victrola began playing music. None of them had done it as they were all together. The frightened teens grabbed their ill-gotten goods and made for the front door. Between the witch's house and the one next door, they saw something moving in the shadows.

It moved into the light of their flashlights. One of the girls screamed as all saw a wolf walking upright just like a human would. It headed toward them, and they all felt it wanted to hurt them. So, they bolted for Jenny's house. Thankfully, the creature never followed them through the woods to the house.

When Jenny tried to tell her mother what they'd done, the teens ended up surrendering the book and other items to the mom. They never learned what happened to the stuff, and they never went back to the witch's house or saw any wolf in the area, upright or on all fours.

Could this have been an animal spirit conjured by a witch to protect the cottage and the items inside? Or maybe it was a witch who shifted into a wolf form?

Werewolves from Outer Space or Other Odd Things

Never moon a wolf.
~Mike Binder

Full moon (Wolf Moon)

There are theories of what dogmen or wolfmen might be, like those connected to

Sasquatch and other cryptids. There's not to say that maybe one of these might be right, but again, until someone proves it, they are still theories or wild ideas, like werewolves from outer space. Or inspiration for some writer to run with and write a short story or novel.

Werewolves from Outer Space

Some stories and theories might have come from left field (or right), and one is never sure what to believe or not. Like the story I discovered about the gentleman who said he had been in contact psychically with werewolf-like aliens until they turned their attention to him the same way. His explanation to the author of *Real Wolfmen* exposed that our planet went through several geographical epochs, and during one of these times, intelligent wolf-headed aliens had landed here. They are biding their time, waiting until our species destroy itself so they can take over the earth. Considering how the current pandemic of Covid can infect our canine companions, plus other animal species, it makes me wonder: do they have a vaccine to protect them so they can survive to take over the planet? But again, maybe Covid came from the aliens. No, too wild.

This man claims that these upright canids resemble Anubis and that their fur contains symbiotic, bioluminescent bacteria, giving a shimmering look to their coat when they move. He said the fur also gave off an unpleasant odor from the bacteria, which released a hydrogen sulfide gas product. These wolf-beings also have a warrior caste that wear a bio-armor beneath their fur, and this explains their bullet tolerance. Their travel mode is portals resembling "cones of darkness," so they can escape capture by humans.

Are these upright dogmen/wolfmen real, flesh-and-blood creatures, or spirit beings from another world? Can these cryptids vanish, using something not unlike aliens in our movies have to escape detection or capture? Or maybe they are using magic, as if they had an invisibility cloak?

Morphing from One Shape to Another Sounds Werewolfish to Me

Even scarier stories tell of werewolf-like creatures that can change their faces, or enter or exit a building without opening a door or window. They are even able to control someone by telepathy, such as what happened to one student of sciences. He was visiting his ex-girlfriend at the time, in the Isthmus section of Madison, Wisconsin. The local history of the area speaks of lake monsters and ghosts. The first settlers found early Indigenous-made mounds here.

After he and his ex-girlfriend went to bed, he got a compulsion to step outdoors. He knew this could mess up any chances of rekindling the flame of his old romance, but he had a compulsion to go out. He found himself walking along the street, between one and two in the morning. Cars still rolled down the road, and streetlights lit up the area, so it wasn't like he was by himself.

He noticed a dark figure about 20 yards ahead. He thought it was another man, like himself, but then it dropped to all fours. Shocked, he understood it was not a human then, but an animal, looking like it might be a dog.

Then it got crazier. It moved quickly but in one spot. The leg movements became lightning-fast, and he began to wonder if it was two dogs coupling. It hit him that it wasn't two animals, but only one, metamorphosing.

The thing turned to look at him, and he saw a dark, hairy body with the head and face of a gorilla. It didn't seem scared of him or the passing traffic, or that he had seen the transformation. Shaken, the student bolted back to his girlfriend's place and pounded on the door, begging her to let him in. When she did open the door finally, she said, "You look like death."

There is an interesting account of shifting from one form to another, written in a book by an author with a Ph.D. in theoretical physics. A researcher told the author that they were watching a person who had swallowed LSD at Brighton, England, in February of 1988. LSD is *lysergic acid diethylamide,* a potent synthetic hallucinogenic drug. Some took it in the 70s and thought they could fly, so that they would jump from windows, but they never flew like a bird; instead, they fell, some to their deaths.

The subject these people watched didn't fly; instead, it morphed into a four-legged animal. Had the drug convinced the mind to change the physical form, or was this otherwise a mass hallucination or intended to be a hoax?

Whatever the case may be, it makes one wonder if the possibility of werewolves or other shapeshifters are more a possibility than we think. It doesn't hurt to wonder.

Dog-faced Creatures in Her Room

What happened to a woman when she was a teenager and lived in the Southeast with her parents? The place was rural, hilly, and wooded.

She awoke and found two upright dog-faced creatures on each side of her bed. Both reminded her of Anubis of Egyptian mythology (although she never read or heard of the mythology of dog-headed gods); they were covered in dark fur at the time of the visitation. She laid still as one of the creatures began walking around her room. Neither threatened her, and she felt they were intelligent but lacking emotion. They did not feel evil, but again, they didn't feel benign, either.

Eventually, they vanished from her room, and she dropped back to sleep.

The next day, nothing appeared missing, nor did any door or window feel like someone had broken inside. The weirdest thing about this event is that she had seen a spirit of a woman in her room, too, but the dog-faced twosome frightened her more.

She never had another visit.

Black Faceless Weredog
Antioch, Illinois

When Beth (not her real name) was 11 years old, she had a scary experience. She came upon a large, black dog and thought it might be her friend's black Labrador, Hoss.

"Hey, Hoss," she called out. "Hey, boy!"

The dog stopped its sniffing and looked up at her. She realized the animal was not Hoss. The impact of its stare bothered her, as it felt both electrifying and horrible at the same time.

The dog thing stood up on its hind legs and morphed into a man whose face did not have any features.

Scared out of her wits, the girl ran to her house and bolted inside, locking the door behind her. Alone in there, she called her friend and begged her to have her dad pick her up. Her friend's father did come to get her. Beth never saw the creature again and was glad she never did.

More Werewolf Stories

I'm hairy on the inside.
~Angela Carter, Company of Wolves.

Werewolf Hollow
Shelbyville, Indiana

Thanks to my friend, Courtney Mroch, for pointing out this interesting spot. There is even, in Shelbyville, Indiana, an area called Werewolf Hollow. It is known for strange creature sightings and unexplained noises at night. Although, the video on YouTube she pointed me to was more about a local legend of the Haunted Twins house in the area, but still, it seems there were werewolf/dogman sightings here as anywhere else.

A Depression Era Werewolf
Chillicothe, Illinois

Back in the 1930s, a farmer and trapper named Jack Ratliff had problems when he found something was stealing animals from his traps. It always occurred during the nights of the full moon. The only evidence he found was a piece of the animal he'd trapped still caught in the trap and bloody footprints of something on two feet.

When trapping season ended, the mysterious thief took to stealing chickens from Ratliff's chicken coop and only leaving spots of the bird's blood on the floor. This only happened when the full moon was in the sky.

Ratliff filled his 12-gauge shotgun with rock-salt shells, grabbed a knife and lantern, and settled down near the hen house to wait.

When squawks from his chickens erupted from the hen house, Ratliff lit the lantern, unlatched the door, set the lantern on a peg, and lifted his gun muzzle to blast whatever was inside.

He found some huge, hairy thing crouching over a dead bird in its paws like a human might. The creature's head had a snout, a ruff of fur not unlike a mane, and pointed ears. Its manlike arms ended in sharp claws at the end of the paws.

The light of lantern hit it, and it dropped its meal. The creature turned to Ratliff and lunged on two feet at him, howling. Ratliff blasted the thing with rock salt and knocked it back. Not for long, as enraged, it went after the human in a second attempted assault.

Ratliff swung the butt of his gun as hard as he could and struck the beast. The monster turned and ran to the back of the hen house. It smashed through the hole it'd already made as an entrance.

From then on, Ratliff was no longer troubled by the creature. Neither were his neighbors, as he learned they, too, had been having the same problems.

Inquiring around, Ratliff learned that after his confrontation that a local person had disappeared. Known as a "pagan hermit," the missing man had lived beneath a bridge. The man practiced magic rituals.

Ratliff began to believe the man had made a pact with the Devil to take an animal form as a werewolf would. After that, Ratliff had some silver bullets, just in case.

Werewolf
Elkton, Maryland

It was close to midnight when a couple driving along Old Field Point Road spied a pair of yellow-green eyes reflecting their headlights. At first, they assumed it must be a deer, as it was high enough above ground level. Until they drew closer and saw a large canine crouched on its hind legs. It held its forelimbs in front of it, instead of on the ground like most four-legged beasts did.

Their headlights revealed it had scruffy, dark-brown fur, with a ruff of fur on the back of its neck. It had the snout of a dog or wolf, and its pointed ears perked up even straighter as it looked at their vehicle. It sat next to a mailbox that was tall enough for a mail truck—and what shook the couple, was that the crouching beast was taller than the mailbox! One thing the wife knew, as someone who worked with dogs professionally all her life, was that this was not a dog. The only dog that might be close to this height was the English Mastiff, and this was not that breed! It was not any of the other biggest breeds, either.

They roared away from the animal and up the road to their house, where they pulled into their driveway, got out, locked the car, and got inside the house.

A friend saw the creature on the same road a year later, reminding them of their own experience that they tried to forget as something they had mistaken. It had its back to the friend, but then, it turned around to show its canine face to her. What scared her was this dog was standing on its hind legs, like a man would. But she didn't run away; instead, it bolted in a hunched over manner.

When her friend told the woman about it, she got chills. For that meant it was still in the neighborhood. Worse, was how much it looked like those werewolves in the movies, and that was scary.

Wolfman on a Sunday Morning
Oroville, California

Security guard Anthony Chaney had driven home to Chino from work one Sunday after one in the morning. Tired after his part-time job in Marysville, he looked forward to bed. Werewolves or anything like that was far from his mind. As his Impala neared Ophir Road, he saw a creature with light fur in the field to his left.

Now seeing a dog or even a coyote wasn't freaky, but one that stood and walked on its hind legs scared him wide awake. It also looked at his car before it finally dropped down to all four and, in several great hops, made its way across the field and into the national forest.

The next time he was at work, he told his coworkers about the "werewolf," and they laughed at him. It didn't stop him from researching any local Indigenous legends. He came across a tale from the Maidu people, who spoke of a Bigfoot-like being who lived in the forest and ate children. The Maidu also believed their shamans could shapeshift and become a bear. No mention of other animals, particularly a wolf.

One colleague at work did not laugh at him because his father saw something like Chaney's wolf on his Oroville ranch in the 1990s. His father was out one night, checking his fence as something seemed to be spooking his cattle. He came upon a 6-foot-tall furry creature standing upright that had glowing red eyes, and he raised his rifle and shot several rounds at it. It took off, and the rancher couldn't find any blood on the ground the next morning.

Scary Wolfman Incident
Okarche, Oklahoma

It was 1993, and the two men had parked their Toyota, windows down, as it was a lovely evening. They talked on several subjects when the driver, Brandon, heard something on his side of the car. He turned his head and found a bipedal, 7-foot black wolf peering through the window at them!

His heart beating like bird wings against a cage, and his breath shucked out of him as he stared at a head with pointed ears and a maw opened to reveal large, sharp fangs. It had red eyes. The creature placed one paw on the roof while the other rested on the bottom of the window's frame. The small car began rocking as it pressed against the side.

Suddenly, the creature looked away, as if something in the distance caught its attention. Brandon felt an overpowering need to make a getaway. So bad that he even tried to climb over his buddy to get out of the passenger window before he realized he couldn't due to being seat belted in.

Brandon tried to turn the key in the ignition with his shaking hand. His friend looked at him oddly as the engine roared to life, and he drove away. Brandon asked his friend, "Did you see it? Did you?"

The friend must not have but still freaked out by Brandon's driving, as he refused to ever go with him in a car again. He had felt the rocking but never saw the animal. As for Brandon, he couldn't even drive in the country at night after that.

He remembered there was intelligence in the creature's eyes, not like an animal at all.

That it could have killed him and his friend if it wanted.

The Teacher and the Wolfman
Ada, Oklahoma

In 2011, a school counselor was driving just after dawn when she spied a man walking to the side of the road behind a fence. As she drew alongside, she saw not a man but a muscular, upright wolf carrying a small deer over its shoulder with ease. It quickly stepped over the fence, crossed the road, and walked into the field on the other side, all on its hind legs.

She never drove down that road again.

Georgia Werewolf

Joel Hurt passed away in 1847, leaving behind four children: Emily Isabelle, Sarah, Mildred Owen, and Alpheus Joel. He also left behind a widow, Mildred, their home, Pleasant Hill, and lots of money. Emily was six at the time. Thinking about what was best for her children, Mildred sent them to a boarding school in Europe. When the kids came home after a semester abroad, Mildred noticed something off about Emily.

The girl seemed to be sick and said she couldn't sleep. Worried about Emily, Mildred kept an eye on her. She discovered that when the girl fell into a deep sleep, she would arise and leave the house, always heading into the nearby woods. When the girl was awake, Mildred asked Emily about it, but the girl said she never remembered any of it. Of course, it could have been sleepwalking, but this was a different time, and they did not know what we now know.

Things got weird.

The girl's appearance began to change. Her teeth sharpened like fangs and hair would sprout in odd places. People began to wonder, as farmers found their livestock slaughtered by what appeared to be a wolf. Red wolves once lived in Georgia, but no one could ever find the wolf that caused these troubles.

People's thoughts went from wolf to werewolf. So, they waited for the next full moon and went hunting for it. They came upon a wolf, the size of a man, that walked on its two hind legs and shot at it. Hit, the wolf yelped and bolted into the woods.

When Mildred heard the gunfire, she rushed to Emily's room, but the girl was not in her bed or anywhere else in the house. She ran outside and found a wounded Emily in the woods. Since it was known that there had been shots fired at a large wolf and folks got wind of Emily being treated by a doctor for her injury, there arose rallying cries of her being a werewolf.

Mildred sent Emily to Europe after the girl got better, hoping that might cure her of werewolfism. The wolf attacks stopped, and when Emily returned home, nothing started up again. Emily lived the rest of her life in peace, became a businesswoman, and passed away at 70 years of age.

Shunka Warak'in
Montana

Since no one has ever seen the Dogman shapeshift, I have decided that adding cryptids or monsters, not unlike a werewolf or shapeshifter, could be added to this book, like the Shunka Warak'in of Montana.

In 1886, a rancher named Israel Ammon Hutchings had shot some dark, wolf-like animal on his property; it had been chasing his wife's geese, but he missed the mark. None of the white people who lived in the area knew what it was, but the local Indigenous tribe did. They called it a Shunka Warak'in, which meant "carries off dogs." Others saw it and described the creature as 48 inches long, not including the tail, plus it stood 28 inches at the shoulder.

It was black, with high shoulders and a back that sloped like a hyena's (I assume somebody had seen the African animal at some time in their life, to say this). This had been included in a book titled *Trails to Nature's Mysteries: The Life of a Working Naturalist* by Hutchings' grandson, Ross Hutchings.

Israel got his chance at the creature again. One morning, his dogs barked at something in alarm, and when he saw it was the cryptid, he took another shot at it, managing to kill it this time. At some point, they donated the dead thing to Joseph Sherwood. Sherwood owned a grocery store, which happened to be a museum at Henry Lake in Idaho. He mounted the carcass and displayed it in the building for many years, calling it a ringdocus.

The creature is now back in the Hutchings family's hands, purchased by another grandson, Jack Kirby, in 2007. Although its DNA has never been tested, as Kirby is resistant to that idea, speculation has the creature pegged as maybe a Borophagus, a hyenalike canine that once roamed North America—at least, back in the

Pleistocene era. That meant it had been extinct since the last Ice Age.

Is it a prehistoric canine, or is it fake? Until Kirby allows DNA testing, we will never know for sure.

Nebraska Wolfman

Nebraska is the state of m y birth. It is a midwestern state on the Great Plains, its capital is Lincoln, and its largest city is Omaha, which is where I was born.

Many settlers built their houses of sod, as hardly any trees grow on the plains, including my father's farming great-grandparents on his father's side. Indigenous peoples, including Omaha, Missouria, Ponca, Pawnee, Otoe, and various branches of the Lakota (Sioux) tribes, lived in the region for thousands of years before European exploration. The state is crossed by many historic trails, including that of the Lewis and Clark Expedition. Nebraska's name is the result of anglicization of the archaic Otoe words *Ñí Brásge*, pronounced ɲĩbɾasˀkɛ (contemporary Otoe *Ñí Bráhge*), or the Omaha *Ní Btháska*, pronounced nĩbɫˤasˀka, meaning "flat water", after the Platte River, which flows through the state.

Nebraska was admitted into the United States in 1867, two years after the end of the American Civil War. The Nebraska Legislature is unlike any other American legislature in that it is unicameral, and its members are elected without any official reference to political party affiliation.

But for me, most of all, it was nice to find a werewolf story connected to the state.

A man claimed to have an encounter with a werewolf while driving on Interstate 83 in the southern part of Nebraska. He'd kept his car at the posted speed after a policeman had stopped him, but when he saw the yellow-eyed canine coming at him from the other side of the highway, he stomped on the gas and left the creature behind. Had he encountered a genuine shapeshifting werewolf or maybe a dogman, or perhaps he imagined it all?

Wolfman of Lawton

The citizens of Lawton witnessed a series of werewolf sightings in the 1970s, during the wintertime. It all began when a man saw a bipedal wolf standing by his fishpond, which brought a heart attack upon him. From then on, more sightings occurred, from the creature leaping over bushes to chasing cars to stalking through the town.

A policeman came to an apartment building after a call from another witness, and he found the beast perched on a railing outside of the man's apartment, 17 feet off the ground. The thing's face looked burned. As soon as it saw him, the creature leaped from the railing to the ground and took off.

Just like you would see in any werewolf movie, the officer noted that torn remnants of clothing hung from its body, as if the person had changed while still dressed.

Dogtown—Home of Werewolves Gloucester, Massachusetts

Once known as the *Common Settlement*, the area later known as Dogtown is divided between the city of Gloucester and the town of Rockport. Dogtown was first settled in 1693, and according to legend, the name of the settlement came from dogs that women kept while their husbands were fighting in the American Revolution. The community grew to be 5 square miles and was an ideal location as it provided protection from pirates and

Indigenous peoples unhappy at losing their land.

By the early 1700s, the land opened up to individual settlement as previously it had been used as common land for wood, and pasturing cattle and sheep. It is estimated that at one point 60 to 80 homes stood in Dogtown at its peak population. In the mid-1700s, as many as a hundred families inhabited Dogtown, and the number of inhabitants remained steady until after the American Revolution.

Various factors led to the demise of Dogtown, including a revived fishing industry from Gloucester Harbor after the end of the American Revolution. The area had become safe again from enemy ships, which allowed cargo to move in and out of the new fishing port. The success gave way to international shipping, including timber, and quarried rock. New coastal roads were built that also contributed to Dogtown's demise, as these roads ran past the town to Gloucester, which at the time was booming.

Most of the farmers in the town moved away by the end of the War of 1812, as Dogtown had become a risk for coastal bombardment. Dogtown eventually became an embarrassment with its dwindled reputation, and some of its last occupants were suspected of practicing witchcraft.

As the last inhabitants died, their pets became feral, possibly giving rise to the nickname "Dogtown." The village was all but abandoned by 1828. The last resident of Dogtown was a freedman named Cornelius "Black Neil" Finson, living in a cellar-hole in 1830. He was removed and taken to a poor house in Gloucester. The last structure in Dogtown was razed in 1845, ending what had once been a thriving community.

Most of the area of Dogtown is now a dense woodland, crisscrossed and bisected by trails and old roads. Dogtown Road is off Cherry Street in the western section (the Gloucester side) and is lined with the remains of the cellar holes of the settlers, many of which are numbered in correspondence with names from John J. Babson's book of the history of Gloucester.

Most of the land is held in trust by Gloucester and Rockport and is therefore protected in perpetuity. The current state of Dogtown affords rich recreation opportunities to hikers and bikers, dog walkers, nature lovers, cross-country skiers, geologists, and historians. The area is peppered with house-sized boulders, including one named "The Whale's Jaw," which it resembled before collapsing after a picnic campfire got out of control in 1989.

The northwest corner of Dogtown is known as the Norton Memorial Forest and covers 121 acres. This land is named for Frederick Norton, a NASA physicist and MIT professor, whose family-owned land on the outskirts of Dogtown.

Dogtown is also named for more than witches in its history, being great recreation area, and history, it seems it is also known for werewolves.

Werewolves of Dogtown

Dogtown was noted for witches; one of those witches shapeshifted into a crow. But witches were not the only things people feared in this now-deserted village.

Rumor spoke that some of the folk in the shunned place might be werewolves. Sights of wolf-like creatures over the years in the past could be said to be myth or folktales, except even today, there are reliable witnesses talking of seeing creatures with wolf heads.

Could these be dogmen?

One sighting happened on March 17, 1984. The witness was David Myska of Allston, and his encounter happened at six that evening. A full moon rose over the Annisquam River at the Crane's Beach Reservation. A large creature roamed the cliffs above the dunes of the riverside.

David reported it to the Ipswich police, saying either a dog or cat, and thinking maybe a mountain lion, as it appeared larger than any dog, wolf, or coyote he knew. Problem with it being a cougar: it had been two centuries since anyone had seen one in the state.

They found a deer killed 4 days later. Its throat was slashed, and claw marks grooved into its head and chest. Terribly mutilated, and yet, it appeared the flesh had not been eaten. It seemed that this animal just thirsted for blood, nothing more.

The same night, two teens saw a monstrous gray canine with large fangs foaming at the mouth loping into the woods. Dogtown overlooks the reservation, and where the teens saw the creature, the street led into Dogtown.

Werewolves of Pennsylvania

In Pennsylvania, the first werewolf story I found went back to the late 1800s when a hunter shot a 7-foot-tall, bipedal wolf. Afterward, the hunter approached the carcass, finding a dead, naked man.

That must have been a shocker.

Over the years, witnesses noticed wolfmen to dogs standing on two hind legs, to wolves with human faces. One such encounter happened in Mercer County in 1990 and was reported to the Dogman Field Research Organization. Some friends were walking in the woods near their homes when they heard a sound. When the people shone their flashlight in the direction of where the sound came from, they saw a huge dog eating something on the ground.

The canine stopped and whipped its head up. It rose to its hind feet and glared at them before it dashed into the trees. What struck them most was that the creature didn't have a doggish body, but more like a man's body, covered in fur. Its head had pointed ears with a snout like a wolf's or a dog's. A couple of them returned the next day during daylight and found a half-eaten deer lying where the wolfman had been.

Wild Man or Wolfman
McNairy County

I am adding this, as wild man encounters might be attributed to both Bigfoot lore and werewolf legends. Such as the wild man encounters in McNairy County in the 1800s and later, up to modern times, in other counties. The last recorded appearance was in the 1990s in Carter County, a good distance from McNairy County.

This being is reported to have dark gray or dark red hair and stands at 7 feet tall, with scary red eyes. Its beard and hair hung to its waist.

The differences in hair color suggest either more than one Wild Man, or was it the same Wild Man but aging since the 1800s, although witnesses claimed it to be fast and strong? People said its screams could bring a chill. It focused many of its attacks on women, although none of those attacks succeeded, as reported by the *Hagerstown Mail's* May 5, 1971 edition. It approached homes, too, but then it would take off running and leap over fences to vanish.

Well-known paranormal investigator Robb Phillips, who appeared in the *Monsters and Mysteries in America* paranormal reality TV show, described his own encounter with the Wild Man at Watauga Cliffs.

It was raining as he hiked with his cousin toward the cliffs, and he and his cousin froze when they felt the mood in the forest change. In his interview in the Elizabethton newspaper, he said, "Everything stopped, and there was no sound. Suddenly, we heard twigs snapping, followed by a scream that neither sounded human nor animal. Scared, we both bolted."

But as they fled, they did see what caused the scream: A very tall beast with red eyes standing there beside a tree. Its odor stank.

Hairy Man or Wolfman Marion County

This matches the wild man seen in the story just related. One woman was exploring a cave and saw something climbing a wall in there. It had brown eyes, completely covered in brown hair, and had paws at the end of its arms and legs.

A group of people walking in Marion County's woods also reported something like what the woman saw in the cave. It approached them on the trail, and when it looked up at them, they saw it had a human face!

Wolf Woman
Mobile, Alabama

The half-wolf, half-woman creature frightened the citizenry of Mobile enough that people began calling *The Press-Register* to give their stories of the sightings. On April 8, 1971, the newspaper reported the phenomenon, complete with a drawing of the creature conceived by a newspaper illustrator: "Listening to as many as fifty phone calls the Press-Register had received, day and night, in approximately a week, you wonder if perhaps there isn't something out there."

Witnesses described the creature as "pretty and hairy," and "the top half was a woman and the bottom of a wolf." An unnamed teenager got quoted as saying: "My daddy saw it down in a marsh, and it chased him home. Now, my mommy keeps all the doors and windows locked." Another witness heard the creature had escaped from a circus sideshow.

The reporter said the fear of witnesses seemed real, although the initial reports would have begun on April Fool's Day. The police were getting calls, too, and although officers would not make an official comment, they did investigate to determine what, exactly, Mobile's citizens were seeing.

Sightings of half-wolf, half-human creatures have been reported throughout history, with the werewolf being the most common incarnation. The legends of anthropomorphic animals stem from Indigenous folklore and capture the imagination. Within days, sightings of the Wolf Woman of Mobile stopped and none have been reported ever since.

The Downey Booger
Winston County, Alabama

West Virginia is not the only state that has the Downey Booger, so does Alabama. In the later part of the 1800s, Winston County was known for the Downey Booger.

Cousins John and Joe Downey returned home from a community dance one night when they saw the creature. John and Joe rode their thoroughbreds, recounting the events of the evening, when suddenly a strange-looking creature, bearing the resemblance of both a human and an animal, leaped out in front of them. They made their horses turnabout and galloped opposite of where they lived.

Suddenly, the horses came to an abrupt stop. The men kicked them in the side, beat them with the reins, yelled, but the horses wouldn't budge an inch. Finally, they got their mounts to turn around, and they rode back home, remembering a longer route they could take."

One moonlit night in early fall, Jim Jackson loaded his two-horse wagon with his homemade moonshine barrels. He climbed in the wagon and snapped the reins, and his team took off. Jim was heading for the commissary in Galloway, a mining town a few miles from his home. As he glanced back over his right shoulder, he spied a peculiar-looking wolfish creature following his wagon. His first impulse was to try to outrun it, but he remembered his gun on the wagon seat beside him. Jim grabbed the revolver, aimed, and fired twice. It screamed like a woman in distress and went limping away on three feet.

The news spread that Jim Jackson had shot the Downey Booger, and they formed a posse to search for it. People combed the forest, only finding traces of blood leading to a distant cliff.

Was the Downey Booger a werewolf, dogman, or something else? What the Downey Booger actually was will forever be a mystery.

The White Thing
West Virginia

Some descriptions of the White Thing have it killing like a werewolf. The only difference is it has white hair or fur. Is it an albino werewolf? There are reports of this creature in other states, but most reports come from West Virginia.

One man in the state encountered a White Thing as a young boy in woods near his home and described it like a cross between a wolf and a lion, with long, shaggy white hair.

Descriptions of this creature made by others have it with enormous jaws and fangs and that it screams like a terrified woman in pain. And that it attacks in a ferocious manner. Victims claim they can feel it tearing into their flesh, but when suddenly the beasts are gone, they find nothing wrong. Although there have been victims that were killed, their bodies were found bloodless and torn up badly.

Bullets appear to have no effect on these creatures. The White Thing also has an aversion to graveyards. This means this might be the best place to run to if you are being chased by one of these monsters.

One man, Frank Kozul, who immigrated from Croatia, was walking home after his shift at the coal mine late one night in July 1929 when he had a run in with the White Thing. He later described it as 4 feet at shoulder height and that it looked like a large, white, shaggy dog with oversized jaws and a bushy tail. It sprang at him, growling and snapping its jaws. Kozul threw his pail at it, but it went through the creature as if it was a ghost. The man turned around and ran for his life, but it slammed into him. His hand pushed at it but passed though as if nothing was there. He fell against a headstone of a grave. Suddenly, not hearing anything, he looked up and found that the creature had vanished. Checking himself, he didn't find any bite marks or scratches on him, or his clothes ripped.

In the 1970s, hunters encountered a White Thing that leaped from some brush, knocking one of the men down. The others ran away, but they returned to help their friend. They found him on the ground on his back. He was screaming that it was tearing into him, ripping his entrails from his body, but not a scratch or bite marred him, and the White Thing had disappeared.

A West Virginia folklorist, Ruth Ann Musick, collected folktales where this beast had killed and mutilated many horses and sheep. So, humans are never harmed in the tales told, but it's apparently not the same for farm animals.

Whatever these White Things were, whether related to the dogmen, in being dog-like and able to walk on all fours or their hind legs, a werewolf, or something else, I figure they belong in this book because like dogmen, it makes me wonder what were werewolves that people saw them as far back as prehistoric times.

Wolfman in the Chicken House Brownington, Missouri

When Christi was a young girl in Brownington, she and her sisters were heading back to the house from the outhouse when they saw something in their backyard. It stopped and turned to look at them. It looked like something out of a werewolf horror movie! Suddenly, it took off. When they went into the house and told their parents about what they saw, the adults thought they were making it up.

The next morning, their mother had the girls go to the chicken coop to collect eggs for the family's breakfast. They found six of the chickens with their heads ripped off. For the next month the family kept hearing noises outside the house and whenever the father rushed out, he found nothing. The family sold the farm and moved a month later. People claimed what they saw was the Missouri monster, MO MO, but as Christi said, it looked just like a werewolf and not some sasquatch.

Arizona's Werewolf Story
Tempe

One would never think in the middle of a town like Tempe, Arizona, to encounter a werewolf.

But it happened.

In 2009, four teens—boys and girls—left a Bible study meeting out of boredom and were walking the Shalimar Golf Course when one of the gierls shouted out that 'something jumped down from a palm tree.'

Now, the palm trees on this golf course stood about 35 feet tall, and the others just laughed as they thought maybe she saw a palm come loose and fall to the ground.

Suddenly, the girl screamed.

When one of the boys turned to her, he saw something he couldn't believe: Something huge and furry, hunched over and blacker than the night itself, was heading toward the teens along a wall. It looked to be as tall as him, and he was 6 feet tall at the time.

The kids bolted back to the building they had been in earlier, no longer bored, and scared stiff.

When the meeting dispersed and the teens had to go back outside, they didn't see the creature anywhere. None of them ever encountered it ever again.

DOGMEN

*Somewhere in the Northwoods' darkness a
creature walks upright
And the best advice you may ever get is don't
go out at night!*
~Steve Cook, *The Legend of Dogman*

The Dogman

*The beast may go all the way back to the very
first settlers in Wisconsin,
who described canine creatures who would
attack and then vanish without a trace.*
~Unknown

You might be asking why I am putting a separate section for the Dogman, when in your mind it obviously belongs with the werewolves. I've done this because though the descriptions of it shout werewolf, there are those investigators who say it has a shorter snout than a wolf has, and that they are dogmen. Now, I would disagree, as I owned a Siberian husky with the same length of snout a timber wolf in our own Metro Richmond Zoo has.

I won't argue, but just give the Dogman its own section in this book.

Dogman describes a group of more than one type of cryptozoological beings that are large and sometimes described as looking like upright canids. Whatever you call them, creatures that look like a perfect cross between man and wolf have been a part of American lore for ages.

I found there are maybe seven different kinds of dogmen that witnesses have encountered. Some even wondered if they were a different kind of sasquatch.

The Seven Types of Dogman:

- Type 3-Variant 1: Tall, lean, and with a baboon head (Devil Monkeys? Because the description of Devil Monkeys reminds me of baboons.)
- Type 3, Variant 2: Hominid body, head like a Chow's.
- Type 3, Variant 3: Sasquatch with a muzzle.
- Canine Variant 1: Like a standing timber wolf.
- Canine Variant 2: Hyena-like.
- Canine Variant 3: Large, strong-bodied, pointed ears.
- Canine Variant 4: Like Canine-Variant 3, but with a much larger head.

For the most part, humanity accepts that dogmen simply don't exist. Though they're generally written off as Hollywood kitsch, people still regularly see them in almost every part of the country.

It would be easy to think that you can rule out the possibility of having a dogman encounter if you don't live in a rural area. It's simply not true, as there have been encounters within city limits or major metropolitan areas. Dogmen have been reported inside the city limits of Cincinnati; Dallas; Chicago; Columbus, Ohio; and several other large cities. More than one eyewitness has claimed to have a brush with a dogman in Central Park in New York City of all places! You can find a map of these sightings at https://www.google.com/maps/d/viewer?mid=1 86_7hq4gxioA6hHZLmaWpCJWCng&hl=en_US &ll=24.208305774880824%2C-37.30046613947561&z=2.

People believe dogmen are only out at night, but there have been more daytime encounters than night ones. A few people have been attacked, but most witnesses have walked away unscathed after running across a dogman. And dogmen are not only in the United States, but have been seen in every place on Earth, except for Antarctica.

What can we glean from these strange sightings? Let's look at a few confrontations to find out.

On Reddit (I won't use the log-on name she uses), one user claimed her relatives saw a "Bigfoot mixed with a wolf" during a brief hunting trip in the woods. After the sighting, her family was so panicked that they refused to let her go outside alone and insisted on teaching her how to shoot a gun.

This could be chalked up to just seeing things, but it's not possible to explain how wolf tracks twice the size of normal were found on the ground. Eerier still, the Michigan Dogman they saw apparently left claw marks on trees as high as 8 feet from the ground!

Another woman on Reddit went for a walk with her dog one night, when suddenly, she was accosted by what she called "a wolfman." She said it had gold-red eyes and it growled at her. She picked up her tiny dog and ran. The creature chased after her, so, she kept running until she could no longer hear it behind her. But by the time she checked to see, she had unlocked her front door and darted inside, setting the locks.

Another Reddit user awoke from sleep one night when he heard a noise. His heart nearly stopped when he saw a dog peering through his window. The man claimed that it had to be at least 7 or 8 feet tall, as the window stood nearly that height from the ground. The beast stared directly at him, and he quickly pulled the curtains close, before ducking beneath his covers. He stayed there until morning, as he swore he heard what sounded like the panting of a canine when he woke up. After a few minutes, the sounds stopped and when he looked at his window, there was nothing there. The man got out of bed, pulled back a part of a curtain panel and saw nothing in the yard.

One theory about dogmen, sasquatch, and other such cryptids, is that they might be from another dimension, maybe even from another planet, that they can suddenly disappear, as if stepping into an invisible doorway or a wormhole. One woman's experience with a Dogman seems to say something about that being a good theory.

One woman had just gotten into her car, when she looked in the rearview mirror, and saw a bipedal, black dog walking behind her car. The creature looked at her, but continued to walk to a tree, where it vanished into thin air.

Could this dogman be from another dimension that just dropped by, or maybe beamed up to a spaceship? Maybe, maybe not.

Others believe dogmen might be something evil, that maybe they are hellhounds or another kind of demon. On a podcast, a former soldier was traveling with his girlfriend when both saw a very big, dark-furred creature running across the road, and the man had to jam his foot on the brakes. They thought it was a bear at first, but bears cannot run on its hind legs for long like this thing did. It stopped and looked at the car, growling. The man said what unnerved him was that what he now realized looked like a werewolf, had glowing red eyes that had glared at him.

Frightened, he roared the car past it and didn't stop for a long time.

Beast of Bray Road and Other Dogmen Wisconsin

What is the Beast of Bray Road of Elkhorn, Wisconsin, and even the Michigan Dogman and other upright canines people have seen? *The Beast of Bray Road*, as written about by Linda S. Godfrey, became the first time anything was printed about the enigmatic dogman. Except she called it as a werewolf. Godfrey talked to hundreds of people who had witnessed it and other beings like it.

Godfrey thought that it could be a species of wolf that adapted over time to walk bipedally, and because it walked upright, an intelligence like that of humans had come into being. As she said, "In general, freeing your forelimbs for those purposes will build up parts of the brain that wouldn't otherwise. And they say that is one factor that made humans smarter, so why wouldn't that make canines smarter, too?"

She also believed they could come from another dimension or the spirit world. Maybe she's right, or maybe it is something else. Maybe even shapeshifters? Maybe aliens? Until we have one that we can touch, and all have seen it, we will never know for sure.

But stories of sightings of the cryptid have been told for a long time.

Some of the first Europeans who settled Wisconsin in the mid-1800s were German. And one knows well that Germany has many werewolf stories. Not long after them, Scandinavians, Belgians, Swiss, the Dutch, and the Irish made their homes in the state. All had their own werewolf stories.

In addition, the Indigenous Peoples there had their own tales of wolfmen and other shapeshifters. The first story about a werewolf sighting was printed in Wisconsin, is famous for its cheese, but also for the Beast of Bray Road. Sightings of this beast, or maybe even werewolves, were first written about in 1930. When a man driving in Jefferson County noticed someone digging in a field he was almost coming upon. Except, as he drew near, he saw it wasn't human when it stood up. The man later described the thing as covered in hair, and a cross between a wolf and an ape. From the description, one could say maybe he'd just seen *The Wolfman* movie in a theater, except that film didn't come out until the 1940s. He also mentioned it didn't have paws, but hands.

This creature continued to be seen, the next time in the early 1960s, when something darted across the road in front of a vehicle in the same county. The driver said it was covered in brown fur or hair, sprinted on two legs and not four, and that it had the head of a dog or wolf. It leaped over a fence and kept running across a field until it was out of sight.

Whatever this was, it would be seen again and again throughout the 1960s and 1970s. Then in 1989, in the town of Elkhorn, south of

Jefferson County, the Beast of Bray Road firmly took life. A dairy farmer saw it on his property; a woman named Lorraine Endrizzi saw a person on the road, but as she drove closer, she saw it wasn't anything human. Tall and hairy, it had yellow eyes and a wolfish face with sharp fangs.

Then, another driver saw it on Bray Road. A girl saw a dog walking on its hind legs across her parents' property near Bray Road. Sights continued through the 1990s, but it was after Halloween 1999, that the Beast of Bray Road became famous.

On the night of Halloween 1999, 18-year-old Doristine Gipson, was driving down Bray Road when her car struck something. Thinking it was most likely a deer, she stopped the car and got out to see the damage. Instead, she saw something that might be more at home in *The Howling,* and not in the rural community. The "werewolf" charged her, and she leaped back into her car, roaring away from the monster. It chased after the vehicle, even jumped on to it, but could not stay on, and landed back on the pavement. The frightened young woman reported the incident to the police. In turn, they told it to reporter Linda Godfrey, who covered the story. From there, she went on to write about Bray Road's famous (or infamous, depending how you look at it) werewolf.

But the Beast or Dogman, whatever you call it, have been seen way before the stories Linda Godfrey wrote about. Such as the one Mark Schackelman experienced when he worked as a security guard for the St. Coletta School for Exceptional Children in Jefferson, Wisconsin in 1936. It became knowledge six decades later by his son, Joe Schackelman, when on his deathbed the old man made the confession about his encounter and Joe drew a picture what his father had seen.

It happened one evening when Mark was strolling the 174 acres of the school. Now way before the building had been built, it was used by the local Indigenous Peoples, for burial mounds dotted the land. And just 5 to 6 miles away, lay flat-topped earthen pyramids, in what is now Aztalan State Park. It was on one of these mounds behind the main building that Mark detected movement and, drawing closer, he saw what looked like an animal digging in the earth.

He noticed that it had dark fur, was the size of a man, and kneeled down in a manner that a four-footed creature shouldn't have been able to do naturally. It fled on two feet and not four, too.

The next day, the watchman checked out the mound in daylight. The dirt appeared to have been torn, as if by claw marks, in slashes of three.

So, that night, he took a big, club-like flashlight while doing his rounds. Once again, he caught the beast on the mound, digging away. But when it stood up on its hind legs and turned to face him, Mark flashed his light at it. He found a creature that stood eyeball to eyeball with him, making it 6 feet, 1-inch, as that was what Mark was. Worse, the stink of rotten meat issued from it.

Not letting himself grow frightened, Mark continued shining his light at it, to get further description of it. He saw that, although covered in fur, it had powerful arms that ended in hands with thumbs and pinky fingers smaller than the middle three digits. That explained the three slashes in the dirt he had found during the daytime. The creature had a muscular torso and a head with a muzzle and pointed ears like a wolf. It growled what sounded like a vocalization, sounding like three syllables, "ga-dar-rah."

As it kept eye contact with Mark, the man felt fear that he might be in danger from it. But it turned and walked away on two legs into the darkness. The nasty odor lingered long after it had vanished. Maybe as a way of leaving a scent, like animals leave when marking territory or defiance? Although Mark worked a few more years at St. Colette, he never saw the 'wolfman' again.

Mark only related his encounter to his wife, Flora. She asked that he never speak of it to anyone else.

In 1958, Mark developed an esophageal hernia that had ruptured and needed surgery, and feeling it might be the end for him, he wanted to get the story of this encounter off his chest. Flora had passed away a few years before, so he called for his son, Joe.

He told Joe of his nightmarish encounter at St Colette's. Joe happened to be a journalist and editor of the *Labor Paper* in Kenosha, Wisconsin. He took not only notes, but even made a sketch of the beast. The drawing would be improved on, as his father would correct some things about it until he felt satisfied with the way the wolfman looked. Just like his father, Joe kept quiet about it, only mentioning it to a few members of his family. He believed his father had seen what he said he saw, as he knew him as a devout Catholic and former heavyweight boxer who never told tall tales. And although what Joe drew didn't have a tail, Joe said his father never mentioned the tail. It was a dark night and Mark faced the creature head on. Even when it ran from him, the bottom half was obscured by the darkness.

The area where St Colette's was located was considered holy long before the Catholic organization owned it, but by the Indigenous Peoples of the area who made the burial mounds. With the connection to Indigenous Peoples, it reminds one of the Navajo and the skinwalkers. Are dogmen more like that than a werewolf? Or maybe just an unknown species? Or was it a denizen straight from Hell, as Mark described to Joe, telling his son that the way it locked eyes with him was more than an alpha animal intimidating him, more personal than a normal wild animal's behavior, like sending a mental message of "You can't get me," like future witnesses would also relate.

Mark Scheckelman's bizarre brush became the first of what would be a wave of such confrontations with human-sized canines nationwide. Always described the same, with a wolflike head, and except for elongated paws, fur, and dog-shaped limbs, it looked humanlike with a muscular torso and shoulders. The problem having human portions of the body is most quadrupeds do not have the shoulder structure a human has, for us to have a wide range of arm movement.

Another thing Linda S. Godfrey mentioned in *Real Wolfmen*, is that the sightings are always near or in marshlands, meaning that maybe the dogmen needed the water, whether for drinking or something else. Jefferson itself is built where two rivers join; a configuration considered sacred by many Indigenous Peoples in the Americas and around the world.

To prove or disprove that Mark Schackelman, or his son, was pulling legs, it is noted that Mark never told anyone else of his encounter and stayed devout, while Joe even published a book titled *God Lives*, nothing close to monsters and monster stories. Joe did publish his father's story, but only much later, after sightings of the Breast of Bray Road was let out of the bag by many other sightings.

Another odd coincidence to Mark's werewolf sighting was that an exorcism had been performed 50 years before that in Jefferson. A priest, Father Friedl, served at the St, Lawrence Parish Church in the 1888s. A family who were congregants approached him, as they felt one of their children, a boy, was possessed. He manifested uncontrollable fits and screamed profanities in a strange voice. As Father Friedl did the exorcism, the boy screamed at him, even calling him 'a red-haired bastard.' Eventually, the exorcism appeared to work, and the boy was cured and lived the rest of his life in a normal manner.

But it was said that the priest himself was bothered by poltergeist manifestations, such as being pushed out of his bed. Finally, Father Friedl left Jefferson for another assignment, only to return in 1890. He died in 1894.

To this day, people are still closemouthed about the boy's or the family's identity. Had the priest really cast a demon from the boy only to have it harass him in turn, or did it become the wolflike beast seen on St Colette's grounds? Or again, maybe this was speculation of two different instances that may not even have a connection, except for the town.

Interesting is the sound the beast made, which was Gadarrah. If spelled like Gadara, that was the name of a region in ancient Judea, 6 miles away from Galilee. In the New Testament, Matthew mentioned that two men living in seaside caves were possessed by demons. Jesus Christ cast the demonic entities into a herd of swine, which then ran into the sea and drowned themselves. But again, Gadara might be nothing more than an animal's growl.

One woman in Hartland had an encounter with a canine-like creature that began one night when her barking dog woke her up. Believing that the animal needed to go outside to do its business, she let it out the door onto her back deck. Instead of running down the steps to the grass of her backyard, the dog stayed behind her and stopped its yapping.

As her deck lights had come on and lent a glow to the yard, besides lights from nearby homes and streetlights on her street out front, she noticed a furry "something" by her trees. It had come from a thicket from the back of her neighbor's yard into hers. Thinking it was a person in a gray jacket at first, she changed her opinion was she realized the figure was not human. It had sharp, pointed ears at the top of its head, a short snout like boxer-type dogs would have, and was covered in gray fur. Instead of hands at the end of the long arms hanging at its sides, there were paws with claws. It walked upright, and it did so on its pads and not flat-footed like a human would. It had a thicker chest, which she had mistaken for a jacket, except now it obviously wasn't. She figured it must be 6-foot due to a branch of a tree it passed under.

Suddenly, it turned its head as if it knew she was watching it. Its face was in shadows due to the trees even with the light and she couldn't see its eyes or even reflected eye shine one sees in animals. As if it didn't care, the creature resumed walking toward the yard next to hers.

Scared out of her wits, she grabbed her dog and bolted inside, locking her door behind her before rushing to her bedroom. Not getting much sleep, she called the police. The officer who answered said he'd believed her and told her to be cautious. He didn't crack a joke about it or say maybe she'd seen a bear or just someone's big dog. She suspected that maybe other people had called in before her by the way he acted, although he never said anything else to the contrary.

Interestingly, the woman told the person she'd called who was investigating her strange matter that her special needs child had been telling her that she had a 'monster' staring through her bedroom window at night and she thought the child was imagining it, but now she understood the child hadn't.

There had been another incident resembling something like this wolf-thing from 3 years earlier. It had been a white, blue-eyed canine that walked on all fours up to a woman's patio door, to keep staring at her in her hot tub. It didn't walk on its hind legs, but she thought it might have been 3 feet high at its shoulders. After a few minutes, it wandered away.

I wonder, as an owner of one in the past, if that wasn't a Siberian husky, as they can have white fur and have blue eyes and is not a wolf. My dog was as big as a Malamute (another large husky breed), or this animal could have been a hybrid, meaning it had wolf in it as well as husky.

The woman tried using a trail camera to captured pictures, but its batteries always seem to be dead the next morning and there was nothing in the camera, picture wise. She had seen, at another time, something standing beneath her neighbor's tree at night when she had let her dog out and hustled her animal back indoors. There had even been the sounds of someone walking on their deck, and when her husband checked, he had found nothing.

Once again, the trail camera's batteries were dead. As for the investigator she'd called, that person checked to see how much wooded landscape was there and found quite a bit, enough for something like a wolfman to use for cover until it got to nearby US Highway 16 to escape to a more rural area.

Before anyone wonders about the full moon aspect, the investigator had noted the moon was waning three-quarters or less. More fascinating to me, is when the woman's trail camera did work and captured something, it was mist, and that her daughter complained of a 'ghost' in her room for a while.

Puppy or Something Else
Milwaukee

In December 2000, two teenage sisters and a younger female cousin checked out the Wisconsin Humane Society for a dog or puppy. It proved fruitless, so they drove home.

As they did so, Maddy, the youngest, 12-year-old cousin caught sight of what looked like a dog sitting alongside the road, on the grass of the cloverleaf. She convinced them to pull over so they could go "rescue" the animal.

Tiffany was driving the car and did as her cousin begged of her. It was as Tiffany, Maddy, and Erin, the other sister, approached it, that the pup suddenly rose up and ran away on its hind legs! It was then that Tiffany noticed that it was taller than them, about 6 to 7 feet, covered in long black fur, and had a muscular body, and that it might be between 200 to 250 pounds. It appeared to not have a tail. She did notice also that it skipped from foot to foot, covering about 10 to 15 feet at once.

The girls were frightened when they realized it was not a normal dog and ran back to the car.

The Dogman from the Cemetery Kenosha

It seems even cemeteries are not safe from these dogmen/werewolves.

Rick was driving to work along County Highway in October 1984 and had just passed the Green Bay intersection when a large creature burst from the side of the road in front of the vehicle, followed by another, much smaller one, that did the same thing. Both beasts had come from a small cemetery.

Both animals ran on all fours, but they stood taller than the front of his 1978 Caravan Suburban. One had to be at least 7 to 9 feet long, while he estimated that the other had to be three-fifths smaller in length. It looked like they had thick manes of fur that ran along their necks and backs, and no tail that could be seen. These canines had snouts longer than a dog's.

Nervous, Rick locked his car door, but the animals had already crossed the road completely and disappeared into the trees on the other side. He told his wife later about the animals, but never told of his unreasonable feeling of fear and evil about them, or that they were nothing more than dogs. Not until 2003, when he saw some drawings of *The Beast of Bray Road* done by Linda Godfrey and talked to her about his experience.

Kenosha is 50 miles from Elkhorn, where witnesses encountered the Beast of Bray Road. But again, as more and more dogmen or wolfmen are being seen, who's to say that the Beast is it? Or had the man had seen something else?

Bearwolf
Wausau and Hubertus

There are those who witnessed something that looks like a cross of bear and wolf. Burek Avenue in Wausau has long bore the nickname of Bearwolf Road. Why? Because people have seen a bear-like creature that stood upright and had a wolf or dog head, with pointed ears, and not a bear head.

Todd Roll, who used to live in Wausau and grew up hearing stories about this beast, was speaking to some students at Mosinee High School in 2004. Several students told him about the bearwolf, that it was seen near Hatley, 15 miles east of Wausau. Todd didn't think of the bearwolf as an actual animal or cryptid, but more likely a land spirit that assumes several forms. So, a shapeshifter, but more a spirit and not a real, flesh-and-blood thing.

Another such cryptid has been seen in Hubertus. This monster went after a roadkill deer.

Interestingly enough, Godfrey had found out that an animal called an amphicyon. This creature existed about 14 million years ago, it was a robust grizzly with massive jaws, the muzzle and fangs of a wolf, short, muscle-bound legs, and a large, heavy tail. It lived in the Northern Hemisphere.

When I read about this, I decided to google and check it out. Description has it is an extinct genus of large carnivorous, bone-crushing mammals, popularly known as bear-dogs, of the family *Amphicyonidae*, subfamily *Amphicyoninae*, which lived from the Burdigalian Epoch until the late Pliocene, with the creature having bear-like and dog-like features. It was possibility an omnivore, although it probably ate more meat than plants. These bear-dogs, in general, went extinct for a reason: the environment. As the Miocene went on, the climate got drier and drier, promoting faster prey, and making it hard for predators that ambushed to survive. Horses and camels, their main prey, became faster and faster.

Whether a spirit using an animal shape, another kind of dogman, or a prehistoric animal that somehow survived to modern times, maybe even used a time blip to end up in our times, something is supposedly seen in Wausau.

Dogman in Whitewater

When Glenn North was driving with his wife on State Highway 12, on a below-zero night in 1996, he never thought to experience something out of the realm of the ordinary. They were traveling between 55 and 60 miles per hour. They had rolled past the intersection where County Road H met with the highway when, out of nowhere, a large animal leaped from the ditch and zipped on all fours in front of the truck. Glenn was about to stomp on the brake, thinking that there would be no way to avoid a collision, but it ran fast enough to clear to the other side of the road. It had to be running at the very least, 30 to 40 miles per hour. Never slowing down, it cleared the ditch on the other side and might have gone through or over a fence.

In the headlights, even at its speed, he didn't think it had been a farm dog. It appeared taller than a wolf, even on all fours. It had long, shaggy dark fur, a long, sharp muzzle, and pointed ears like a wolf's that laid back against its head. It also seemed thicker than the normal canine around its midsection.

He also didn't believe it to be anything supernatural, but a real creature.

Scary Encounter in the Fog
Fort Atkinson

This military base, no longer functioning as one, has had several dogman encounters nearby. One happened in August 1992 to a teenager, Tom, who was driving his buddy home from a wedding they'd attended. They had the windows down and the music cranked up, and the teen was driving his car slowly, as a heavy fog obscured much of the road. A bump reached their ears over the music, which meant the car had hit something on the passenger side and Tom stopped.

Thinking he'd hit a mailbox, he peered out the window until he saw, not a mailbox, but a massive animal. He saw a hand first, but then saw what it was attached to: a large, furry creature that was definitely not a bear. It stood upright, right next to his car.

The boy reported, "It was big. Its chest was at the top of my car, and the fur looked white or pale gray with black streaks in it, before it withdrew back into the fog and become a faint shadow that showed me how really big it was."

It did have large legs on its lower body, but he didn't get a clear view of its face. His sharpest memory was that arm and hand reaching toward him and his friend. He remembered some sort of sharp nails, the arm long and odd-shaped, and that it had gotten the pinstriping off his car, which he had showed to the author of the book who investigated at the time. There was also a skunky odor lingering on the car.

He took his friend home, then contacted the Jefferson County Sheriff's Department and two officers who stopped about it. The police believed he'd seen a bear, but he said he hadn't.

The same kid, who was driving with another friend, saw a dogman 2 months later along the same highway. They saw clearly an upright being with a dog head and legs, walking between the road and a cornfield. It stepped over something as it entered the cornfield. Upon later investigation, there was a hillock at that spot. It stood a head taller than the stalks of corn, which appeared 6 feet in height.

Was his first encounter Bigfoot, with the hand being seen, and the second one more definitely a dogman? Maybe both cryptids are haunting the area. Who's to say they can't?

Other Dogman Encounters in America

*In '57, a man of cloth found claw marks on an
old church door.
The newspaper said they were made by a dog.
He'd have stood seven-foot-four.*
~Steve Cook, *Legend of the Dogman*

Michigan Dogman

The Michigan Dogman, along with the Beast
of Bray Road in Wisconsin, made the werewolf,
or Dogman, whatever you want to call it,
become famous and out there for people to read
about. There are even legends that say the
Michigan Dogman appears in a 10-year cycle
that falls on years ending in "7".

It is even thought that Michigan werewolves
could be a projection from Indigenous shamans.
French colonists believed otherwise, counting
lycanthropy with evil magic. The shifter would
vanish before someone's eyes, but it always left
something behind.

Such is what happened to a French farmer,
troubled by a *loup-garou* in the Detroit area.
The farmer melted down a saint's medal to craft

a silver bullet. He only managed to shoot off the creature's tail, but the local Indigenous Peoples kept it as a "powerful fetish."

The Detroiters tracked the werewolf to a swamp, finding a demonic footprint on a rock it was last seen standing upon. They even claimed a sulfur spring bubbled up where the fiend disappeared.

Local Algonquin tribes don't believe shapeshifters are evil, like the white men did. An Ojibway tale, "Tale of the Sheem," is about a young boy abandoned by his selfish family. He is trying to survive as winter hits and runs into a pack of wolves who take pity and provide him with food. They even accept him as kin. Because he grows to accept the wolves, the boy transforms into a wolf himself. There is a translation of this in Henry Rowe Schoolcraft's 1856 "Myth of Hiawatha," in the sixth stanza.

Werewolves became something in Michigan when hobby folklorist and production director, Steve Cook, of WTCM in Traverse City, composed a country and western song about an upright wolf that had no fear of humans, from stories he had collected. The sightings began near a lumber camp in Big Rapids, Mecosta, County in the 1880s. In Cook's song, "The Legend," he changed the location to a camp in

Wexford County. He told a reporter of *Traverse City Record Eagle*, that it was similar to the wolfman, but he called it dogman to be more "homey." Cook's song came out as the news reported the Michigan Department of Natural Resources was investigating a mysterious animal attack on a cabin outside of Luthor in Lake County. They found damage to the screen and molding around a door and window, as if the animal tried to get inside. Inspecting animal prints around the area made them conclude it wasn't a bear, but an unknown canine.

You can hear the song at https://www.youtube.com/watch?v=yd5W0iMLL6k.

And so, the term, dogman, was born in 1987. Hearing "The Legend" over the radio caused Robert Fortney to talk about his own encounter with a "dogman," on the banks of the Muskegon River in 1938. He was target shooting when five dogs attacked him. He shot the lead dog, and three of the others bolted back for the woods, but the fifth one, a black dog, didn't immediately run off; it stood up on its hind legs and stared at him. Fortney said that it had slanted, evil eyes and he swore it had an evil grin.

Although it had been years since his encounter, 68 in fact in 1987, Fortney said, "It scared the devil out of me...I wouldn't call it a Dogman. I wouldn't know what to call it."

If it'd happened to me, I would call it scary and weird.

Feral Dogman
Romulus, Michigan

Dogman sightings have been occurring in Michigan since the 1950s. One of these sightings happened in Romulus, to S. Costea and his family.

Costea lived in a farmhouse with his mother, her boyfriend, and his uncle. The farm was surrounded by woods that also blocked them from the nearby major road. Costea remembered a large dog hanging around in the woods, Its upper part reminded him of a German Shepherd, but the lower half was more like a Doberman pincer; it was about the size of a Great Dane. It also had red eyes, something dogs, and even wolves or coyotes, do not have.

The uncle tried to scare or shoo it away, pitching rocks at it and yelling, but instead, the animal would rear on its hind legs and then charge at him on all fours.

They found many of the screens ripped from their windows or screen doors, and worse, many of the chickens and rabbits they kept, dead and torn to bits. That was scary—slightly even more upsetting. But when it spoke one day, that was when it turned to terror.

Costea's mother had opened his window to cool his bedroom off, as it was a hot, muggy summer night. It was when she passed his room on her way to the bathroom and heard him talking to someone, that she opened his door and looked in.

Costea was standing on his bed, looking frightened, and she saw the feral dog standing upright with its head and front paws through the screen. It growled at them. The Mom tossed an empty bottle at it and it left, enabling her to close and lock the window. She hugged her son and tucked him back in bed, but she left his bedroom door open all night.

The next day, the uncle took his shotgun and tracked the animal, and when he saw it, shot at it, but never hit it, as it disappeared back into the trees. Costea and his family never saw the beast again.

Witchy Wolves—Omer Plains

In *Strange Magazine*, David Kulczyk reported in the spring 1996 issue about these dogmen, or as he called them: Witchy Wolves of Omer Plains. These beasts are connected to a local Indigenous Chippewa legend. They are spirit dogs that guard the graves of ancient warriors and attack anybody who dared to approach said graves at night. Teenagers would foolishly attempt to, as rites of passage. These creatures remained invisible and would knock interlopers down to the ground, barking and snarling. Those who did leave their vehicles to check out things had their bodies scratched, and their clothes ripped, their cars and trucks scored, and the roofs dented.

The most frightening thing that scared many happened to be the high-pitched barking laughter coming from everywhere, but from nothing ever seen. Kulczyk reported big, tough guys crying when they talked about their experiences. Whatever it was, it kept many people from going to Omer Plains.

Dogman in *Fortean Times* Article Dayton, Tennessee

With paranormal magazines and websites these days, it is not shocking to mention sightings of a dogman or two, like the encounter Patricia Law had in the early 2000s. It appeared in *The Fortean Times* in 2005.

Patricia was driving home in the predawn hours to Pikesville from her job in a factory in Dayton. The road snaked over a mountainous area of Walden Ridge. A lonely, desolate spot, she hadn't passed anyone else on the road. On occasion, there would be lit-up homes scattered about, but that was it.

She came upon a lone hitchhiker that wore dark pants and a lighter shirt. As she drove past the person, she saw no human head on the body but a wolf one instead. Her heart pounding, she looked back over her shoulder and saw the wolf face again. She nudged the car's speed up and once again checked her rearview mirror. Whatever she had seen, it was no longer there.

Had she seen someone wearing a Halloween mask or a genuine werewolf? Good question. No matter what, she believed she had seen something out of the ordinary.

Dogman by a Creek
Emuckfaw, Alabama

A couple and their teenage son drove along State Highway 22 the night of November 1st. A full moon hung in the clear sky. Nothing appeared out of the ordinary until they reached the Creek War battle site by Emuckfaw Creek: an animal darted across the road in front of their vehicle.

It looked as large as a German Shepherd, but it didn't look like that kind of dog or any kind of dog they knew. The headlights revealed the creature had a long snout with protruding lower fangs and its back limbs were longer than its forelimbs, unlike most four-legged canines. The light also showed a bushy tail and a blend of red, black, and light gray fur. It didn't show fear of the car bearing down on it.

The mother, who was the driver, slowed down to avoid hitting it. The father said it reminded him of a Chupacabra, but the son in the backseat thought it didn't look like anything he saw before, not a dog or even a wolf.

Was it a Dogman or werewolf, or something connected to the terrible battle that happened near there in January 1814? This fight occurred between Andrew Jackson and his forces, and the Creek Nation encamped there. Maybe one of the warriors could have been a shaman who shifted into a wolflike creature to escape the carnage. Or perhaps it has nothing at all to do with the history of the place.

The Dogman Encounter
Lawrence, Kansas

In August 2014, Michael was driving down the road near Lawrence, Kansas, when suddenly, a deer bolted in front of his vehicle. He jammed on the brakes, waiting to see if any more deer would be darting across the road. As he looked at the side the deer had sprung from, he saw red eyes staring at his truck from the woods.

Grabbing a flashlight from the cab, he stabbed the light at the area where he saw the eyes. It was what his light revealed that shocked him. It looked like a dog about the size of a Great Dane, the back legs shorter than the front. But the most surprising thing was it stood upright, like a man. The creature broke eye contact and walked across the road in front of his truck, still on its two legs. It only took the beast three steps to go from one side of the road to the other. Once it made it to the other side, it dropped to all fours and took off into a field, disappearing. No doubt, to catch that deer.

A Dogman Sighting in Oregon

Lately, there have been dogman sightings in Oregon. Unlike other reports, this case describes the creature as a 7-foot-tall biped canine, like the others across the country, but this one has a human-like face; another striking difference is that it never leaves footprints.

The Glowing Dogman
Pennsylvania

An interesting dogman, maybe even a werewolf, seen by a Pennsylvania man, glowed. Both from upstate New York, the man and his wife, were driving through northern Pennsylvania in 1994 when they encountered a strange light. The light appeared to be bobbing down the hill in the woods alongside the road they were on. Thinking it might be an ATV, even part of a procession, he kept his eye on the road while still eyeing the light.

When the light crossed the road in front of his car about 25 yards or so ahead, he was astonished to see a powerfully built bipedal canine running. It looked both ways of the road and stared at his car approaching. It appeared to be 7 to 8 feet tall, and it had a blue light about it. He couldn't tell if it had fur and, if it did, it had to be short, nor did he see a tail. No eyeshine when it looked his way, just that maybe the eyes were black. The Egyptian god of the dead, Anubis, comes to mind, but this creature appeared more like a dog than a jackal.

The exciting thing about it glowing are the theories of dogmen and even sasquatch being able to travel between worlds or dimensions, even like the woman in Hartland, Wisconsin's encounters of mist captured on her camera and her child talking about a ghost in her bedroom. Whether true or not, it is something to ponder.

Dogman and the Religious Woman Pennsylvania

Another encounter happened to a Pennsylvania woman raised in a religious family. She saw a bipedal canine standing at the edge of a pond near her home. She remembered the teaching in religious class that if she ever saw an animal standing like a man, it was the Devil.

Dog Near a Church
East Hanover, New Jersey

Three teens walked home after eating at a nearby restaurant. They cut through the parking lot of a church when they caught sight of a deer lying on the asphalt. They wondered if a car had hit it, and it managed to make it to the parking lot to die. As they drew nearer, the "dead deer" jumped up, scaring the teens. It ran away from them on its two hind legs, and they realized that it wasn't a deer!

One of the kids, named Mike in the story, saw that it had a dog-like head, but the rest of the body looked more like an ape's and it held its forearms by its sides. That was all he took notice of as he bolted, screaming with his friends, down the street.

Great Dane Dogman
McAllen, Texas

Not always, but sometimes, people see dogmen who are far more dog than man, and that do not look like a wolf.

A group of young adults traveling through McAllen caught sight of a black Great Dane by the side of the road, loping at a high speed. That is when things got strange.

The dog stopped in the middle of the road between cars, rose on its hind feet, and walked like a man would across the road, then went back down on all fours to scamper away.

Kentucky Dogwoman and Young Ones
Land Between the Lakes, Kentucky

One of the possible dogman encounters appears to be a dogwoman and her young ones. One gentleman had a meeting with them one night driving on a road in the Land Between the Lakes region in 2002. He'd just left some friends after a weekend of camping when something ran across the street. Thinking it might be a coyote, he realized it couldn't be because it was upright on its hind back paws. He drew to a stop on the asphalt when he caught sight of another such creature, followed by two more like the first ones, trotting to catch up, all on their hind legs.

It hit him that the first one stood about 6 feet in height. The three others were smaller and made noises, much like those puppies would make. He thought about maybe taking a picture, but he decided to drive away when the large one turned around and began snarling.

Next time you run into a dogman, don't assume it is a guy.

Inner City Dogman
Chicago, Illinois

Interestingly, this happened in the inner city in Chicago, and not in the country. This came from online, at a website for dogman encounters, with the person not giving their name on an encounter experienced by his wife in 1973.

His wife, Jane (name I'm giving her to make the story easier to tell) lived in inner-city Chicago and was about 11 years old at the time of her experience. It was summertime, and she was spending the night with her two female cousins, in the basement bedroom of their house.

The family dog awoke them in the early morning, when it was still dark outside, growling. The basement had windows high up. In one window, Jane saw something looking in. She couldn't make out exactly what it was, but there was enough light from a streetlight outside to see the outline and movement of something.

All three girls screamed, which woke up and brought Jane's two older boy cousins down, to see what was going on. The girls told them what they had seen and the boys ran upstairs to throw on their clothes before running outside to investigate.

The boys saw "someone" running away and they chased after him. It took them a minute or so to get a good look at who they were chasing, because of the sparse lighting in the area, but they swore it looked like a large werewolf. They thought it was someone trying to pull a prank; that a man was wearing a very realistic werewolf costume and dismissed any possibility of it being real. They lost sight of it and returned home.

Years later and with all the stories of the dogmen nowadays, the wife wondered if it had been a dogman that she had seen.

Dogman at Night
Woodford County, Illinois

This came from online, from a website collecting dogman encounters, this one from Illinois. The name is not what was signed at the site but one I made up.

Shelly lives in rural Illinois and had been experiencing strange noises and activity around her house for a period of a couple months. Around four in the morning one night, her dog began barking, like she wanted to go out. Before letting the pup out, she flipped on the back flood lights and peered outside. She caught sight of a wolf/dog/man-like thing standing upright in her back yard and looking at the back door.

It had a proportionally huge head, with pointed ears on top and she noticed an amber-colored eye shine. It had a German Shepherd's or a wolf's head, broad shoulders, the torso like a dog's and she thought it also did not have neck. Because of its massive head, it had an extreme, forward-leaning posture of around 60 degrees. It had thick front thighs that angled forward and tapered down to small knees. Below its knees, its lower legs angled back to its hocks, just like those of a dog.

After a few moments of standing there, it turned and walked into the cornfield behind her property. As it walked into the cornfield, she saw it stood taller than the top of the corn stalks, which rose 8 feet high.

Dogman Encounter
Christian County, Illinois

This is about a friend of the anonymous person who posted this online at a website for dogman encounters. The friend (the poster named his friend in the post, but never who he was, just anonymous, so I will call him Jim) had moved south, to work with his uncle. Things didn't work out, so Brian called and wanted to know if Jim would pick him up at the bus station in Springfield. Jim said, "Sure."

The day Brian was to arrive, his bus wasn't due until 1:30 in the afternoon. When the bus finally rolled into the Greyhound station, he was starving, so both young men drove to Steak and Shake. As they ate, some people they knew showed up and they ended up staying to talk with them. Before they left, Brian wanted to see if they could swing by his girlfriend's house before she left for work.

With nothing else to do, Jim said he would. She lived in Assumption. To get there, they headed back to Taylorville, then they had to cut through the country to get to Assumption. To do this, they had to pass Bertinetti Lake. At that time, they had just started developing the place, for housing, so it was semi-rural, with woods around the lake and the road the two were driving along.

Just as they were about to cross a bridge, some huge, canine-type thing came running out of the woods, to their right. There were good-sized, freshly dug ditches on each side of the highway. It leaped over the right ditch, cleared the highway, and landed on the backside of the ditch on the left side of the road. It then bolted into the woods.

It all happened so fast that Jim never had time to hit the brakes. Jim knew people would say they'd only seen a dog, but they both agreed it was bigger than any big dog they'd ever seen. Besides that fact, Jim didn't know of any dog that could jump that far. He remembered it had gray and light brown fur, and appeared massive and muscular, and it jumped and ran on all fours.

Years later, Jim was looking at the Bigfoot Field Research Organization website. He saw there were two sightings that had taken place about a mile to the east, from where Brian's and his encounter happened. When Jim first read one posted report, it related that creature took off running on all fours, and was wolf-like, not at all like a sasquatch. In that sighting, and the one following, the poster stated the sightings happened where Highway 48 crosses the south fork of the Sangamon River. Jim said, if you follow the river back east until you see Lincoln Trail Road, you would come to where the bridge is.

Dogman Encounter
Mercer County, West Virginia

A sighting of a dogman in 2008 occurred at Hill Top Hill in Princeton in Mercery County. The witness said that she had been outside her aunt's house, sitting on the porch with her boyfriend and holding a puppy. Suddenly, something like an exceptionally large, gray dog burst from some brush a hundred yards away, running down a hill. Her one thought was it had a weird nose and was shocked to see it on its hind legs like a man. The creature stopped at a noise she made, then 5 minutes later, it vanished into the woods on the other side.

The creature rose from being on four feet to its full 7 feet on to its hind legs. It stared at them with red eyes. Instead of attacking them as they feared, it walked back into the thicket on its hind legs like a man would. That's when they noticed that its front legs were actually shorter than the back ones, and more like arms.

The couple hurried back down the trail to the young man's car, and drove to tell his father what they had seen. The father knew what they talked about and said it must be like the one that came around his parents' farm, frightening the livestock and looking in the windows.

When they went to look, they didn't find it.

Dogman Encounter
Chesterfield County, Virginia

It was in 1998 when a man driving along a road in Chesterfield County spotted a very large gray, bipedal wolflike creature dragging the carcass of a deer into the tree line from the road. Shaken by what he had seen, he kept driving.

Dog Eat Dog
Danville, Virginia

Another time a dogman was seen in Virginia was in the 1990s in Danville. The police got a call from a woman one night reporting that "something" had taken her dog. When the police officer arrived, he searched the woods, hoping he could find the dog. A crunching noise came to his ears, and he shone his flashlight at where the sound came from. He saw what looked like a very big dog with pointed ears, crouching down like a man would and bent over something that it was apparently eating. The "dog" stopped eating and turned its head toward him. Frightened, he shot at it. The bullet must have hit an eye because the dogman began blinking, then it let loose a howl as it ran away on all fours. The policeman stepped over to what the creature had been gnawing on and found it was the woman's pet dog.

One Woman's sightings as a Child in West Virginia and Later, Arizona

One woman, Christyne, wrote a thin book that you can find on Amazon about her encounters with dogmen. The first one happened to her as a 10-year-old child, when she stayed with her cousin, Sara, and Sara's paramedic husband. She never said the name of the small town they lived in.

Whenever she went outside to play, her cousin told her not to stray too far from the property, and to take the younger of their German Shepherds, Thor, with her, and be back inside by dinner time or way before dark. Like most kids, Christyne didn't listen but forged deep into the woods surrounding her cousins'

land. A terrible smell, like rotting meat, hit her
nose, and when Thor stopped and wouldn't let
her go forward, she saw the dogman.

It stood up on its hind legs. Its massive head
reminded her of Thor's own. It had yellow eyes,
and instead of paws at the end of its muscular
arms, it had hands edged with claws. It stared
at her, even growled, then when voices of men
calling her name came to Christyne's ears, the
creature ran away.

She never said if it ran on its hind leges or
had dropped to all fours to do this. She found
the dogman's den; a large hole dug in the dirt
that was big enough for it, with two half-eaten
pigs that she believed caused the nasty odor
she'd breathed earlier, plus a scattering of
bones of other animals. It frightened her as she
wondered if the wolfman was going to eat her
and ran into the arms of her cousin's husband,
who just walked up with three firefighters from
his station.

That was not the last time Christyne had an
experience with the creature. Much later, when
she agreed to take something to the old lady
that lived down the road from her cousin, she
felt something was following her, but a
squawking turkey flew out of some bushes; she
believed that was it. Then she caught sight of

the giant dog watching her from some trees. The neighbor let her in, and not long into the visit, they spotted the creature looking through one of the windows in the living room at them. It crossed to the door on the porch and began jiggling at the doorknob.

Christyne called the fire department where her cousin's husband worked and got hold of him. They hid in a linen closet until he and others arrived. The beast was nowhere.

Not long after that, she went to stay with her grandparents, then eventually flew back to Arizona and her parents. She had no experiences with the dogman or any other one, not until she was grown up. These newer sightings happened in Arizona.

She was married at the time of her first encounter with a dogman in Arizona. One night, she was driving home when a large buck bounded out of the woods and into her truck. Not dead, it arose in jerky movements, when something larger and on hind legs bolted from the trees and snatched up the thrashing deer into its arms and gave the woman one look with its red eyes before it walked away with its prey back into the forest. She saw it was not a bear and not unlike the dogman of her childhood, except this one had red and not yellow eyes.

The following day, her husband awoke her, demanding what she hit the vehicle with. She said a deer, but he pulled some long gray and black hairs from another section of the truck, saying, "These do not look like they belong to a deer!" Christyne took him to the other side of the vehicle and showed him the crumpling made by the buck.

Her next encounters came after she became an EMT and was separated from her husband, living with a female friend, named Mae. One night, both women heard something walking on their roof, and when Christyne took a rifle upstairs, she saw a dogman out the window. It climbed down to the porch, and she watched as it began to toss things on the porch out to the front yard.

Christyne got downstairs and out of the house to see the creature on the grass, and before it walked away, she saw this one had yellow eyes. She wondered if the one she met in West Virginia had followed her scent out to Arizona, since the other one with the deer had red eyes.

Dogman Sighting in Matanuska Susitna Valley, Alaska

Melissa was traveling on some old road in the Matanuska-Susitna Valley in 1998. Melissa was in her early 20s in 1998, working swing shifts at the time and commuting about 100 miles each way. It usually was around 2 in the morning by the time she got home.

The time she saw the 'monster' (as I call it), happened on the northern-most section of Trunk Road in the Matanuska Valley, almost smack in between the towns of Palmer and Wasilla. It was only about 10 miles from home as she drove on Trunk Road, which was a narrow, two-lane road of nothing but twists and turns. The surrounding terrain is somewhat swampy and thick with black spruce. It was late October; only days before Halloween and no snow on the ground, but cold enough to be wary of ice. She drove her '82 Subaru at 20 MPH around a curve, when the headlights caught a large, dark figure up ahead.

She let off the gas, so she could slow down and hopefully not hit it, thinking it might be a moose. Most know how much damage a deer could do to a vehicle; a moose is much, much larger.

Bear? No, it didn't look like a bear. It appeared tall enough to be a grizzly maybe, but again, it was too slender. There seemed to be spikes running down its neck and back, which may be why Melissa wondered if it might be someone in a costume, pulling a prank on drivers.

As she drew closer, it slipped into a ditch. The light from her headlights revealed a wolf-like muzzle and large, upright ears and that those 'spikes' on its back were, in fact, clumps of fur. Its spine curved in a smooth, very natural-looking way. Because she didn't pay attention to its bottom half as much as the upper part of its body, she couldn't remember anything about its back legs or if it had a tail. The front legs were very 'dog-like,' and they hung down and slightly toward its front, just like a dog might appear standing upright. Which was impossible--right?

While it looked like a canine, there was still something 'off' about it. Given how close to Halloween it was, the woman thought it might be a Halloween prop. Melissa put her foot to the brake, intending to stop and examine it closer.

Suddenly, it turned its head. The pale, off-white glow of its eyeshine in the headlights destroyed any possibility of a human in a costume or a prop.

Melissa stared in shock, her car slowing down when she snapped out of her trance and stomped on the gas. The car fishtailed, and she thought her vehicle would end up in the ditch, but the tires stayed on the pavement, and she sped down the road for home, never looking back to see if it still stood there or even began chasing after her. It must not have, because she made it home and nothing attacked when she parked by her home.

Melissa has only been on that section of road a few times since, never alone and never in the dark. For the next several years of driving that commute, she went 20 miles out of her way to avoid Trunk Road. The thing never made any aggressive moves, but there was something about it that felt very...she didn't know... predatory. Melissa never saw anything remotely like it again and never heard any stories about it in the area.

Beardog or Inuit Evil Spirit
Alaska

Inuit legends describe a wolf-like or dog-like evil spirit of the Nahanni Valley that kills people by biting their heads off. Though the so-called "Headless Valley" lies in Canada, its resident monster has been sighted in Alaska, at least once, by an American mechanic who described it as a "wolf on steroids." And the crew of the American TV show *Alaska Monsters* claims to have narrowly escaped an encounter with the beast.

Cryptozoologists speculate the saberwolf might actually be a remnant population of dire wolves, or even amphicyonids—also called "bear dogs"—of the Eocene. Descriptions of the creature make it sound more like a bear-dog than a wolf, but who can tell with evil spirits, really?

Waheela
Alaska

There is a story of a large, white wolf called the Waheela. It is considerably larger than a regular wolf, with a broad head and much bigger paws. Tracks from it have the toes spaced far apart. Its fur is snow white and long, with its hind legs shorter than its front ones. It is said to be 3-½ to 4 feet tall at the shoulder, and unlike most wolves being pack animals, this one is often alone. This canine roams the far north, away from human civilization.

In Alaska, the Indigenous tales say it is an evil spirit with otherworldly abilities, and there are strange deaths attributed to it.

One cryptozoologist, Ivan Sanderson, heard about a large wolf seen in the Nahanni Valley in Canada. The man who saw it told him that it stood about 3 feet or more at its shoulders, and white fur covered a body that had a big head, short hind legs, and longer forelegs.

Early European trappers in Alaska had reported running across large white wolves. In the 1980s, a hunter hunted in a remote part of Alaska when he encountered a white wolf. The man claimed the animal had a big head, and it was several times larger than any wolf he'd run across before.

Others don't think it is a large wolf or a shifter, or even a dogman, but a bear-dog, a prehistoric bear that once existed 5 million years ago.

Remember, the next time you go hiking or to a national or state park to camp, if you see a wolflike animal suddenly stand upright, walk back to where you came from. That might be a dogman you encountered!

Wolf and Dog Guardians of the Bridge, Crossroads, Bypasses, and Onramps

Every once in a while, one of them would scream again and pull on one of the tent poles, dragging the whole tent a foot or two.
~Dogman Witness

Bridges, crossroads, and other landmarks outside of towns and cities might be considered portals to other worlds. These portals are where creatures like wolfmen or dogmen, plus other cryptids, have been seen worldwide for centuries, and may be used to get to our world. If you have read *NOS4A2* by Joe Hill or seen the television series based on the horror novel, a vampire used a bridge as a portal to come into our world to steal children to take them to Christmas Town in another dimension. It was even used to travel to different times in history. It's as good as an answer for the cryptids, that they are from other dimensions or alternate worlds. Until we learn the truth, it is still an interesting thought.

Wolfman Near Bridge
Sanger, Texas

In 1985, a man was driving in his pickup truck around one in the morning near an old iron bridge in Sanger, when suddenly a large bipedal creature covered in fur stepped off the bridge. It stopped, lit up by the man's headlights. It appeared to him to be maybe around 5 feet tall, the fur a light brown, and it had a wolf's head with eyes that reflected yellow-green. It also stood upright.

Bipedal Canine from the Bypass
Siloam Springs, Arkansas

One night in the early 21st century, when the full moon shone in the night sky, an African American man and his girlfriend drove on a four-lane highway through Siloam Springs. They came up to the bypass over some railroad tracks. Suddenly, something leaped over the rails and bounded across the road and over to the other side.

The moon had lit up the landscape well enough for the woman to see it. "It reminds me of Anubis, that Egyptian god!" she said.

Her boyfriend turned the car around so they could get another glimpse of it, but it had vanished. Both had grown up hearing Indigenous stories about shapeshifters, but this shocked them.

Was it one of those dogmen, or was it a shapeshifter from the tales of the Indigenous tribes they had heard?

Creature by the Jersey Turnpike Bayonne, New Jersey

This story was published in the *Weird N.J.* magazine. Two EMTs, back from a call, took a ramp off the turnpike when suddenly, a large dog with pointed ears crossed in front of them, on all fours, far enough ahead of them for the driver to jam his foot on the brakes. It looked more like a wolf than a dog in their headlights, and its legs appeared larger than normal, plus its eyes gleamed yellow when it turned its head to look at them.

The EMT in the passenger seat was still sleeping through this, so only the driver saw the creature. He had never seen any dog like this thing, as it bounded off to vanish in the night.

Werewolves in Muskogee, Oklahoma

Ed and his family had two different encounters with what appeared to be wolves.

Except these acted out of the norm for a normal wolf.

Except wolves no longer live in Oklahoma, according to the Oklahoma Archeological Survey. The state's bounty hunting decimated the bison population and reduced the deer population, which led to the complete elimination of wolves in the 1930s. Unsubstantiated rumors of wolves still occur in Oklahoma, says the *Oklahoma State Game Wardens Association Magazine*.

Before the mid-1800s, Oklahoma had a healthy red wolf population. In 1980, the U.S. Fish and Wildlife Service caught the last red wolves in Oklahoma to use them as part of a breeding program designed to save the species from worldwide extinction, but their numbers never recovered, and they went extinct there.

But none of the wolves were gray or black, as in the stories told in the next few paragraphs.

The first sighting occurred in 2006, near the Chandler ramp that Ed took to enter the Muskogee Turnpike. It was night, and he saw a large, gray wolf gnawing on a dead deer. It stopped eating and looked up at the car. He didn't think any more about it, not until his fiancée told him she had seen a large, black wolf eating a deer carcass, except it brought a chunk of the meat to its maw by using its paw just as a human or ape eating food would!

It seemed that those in Ed's family hadn't seen the last of these "wolves," as a family member of his sister-in-law and her friend who was driving the car came upon a big, black wolf on that same ramp. It looked at her with glowing, red eyes; not the ordinary eyes of an average canine, but like those of a hellhound, as they told Ed's sister-in-law!

The relative screamed at her friend. "Drive, just keep driving!"

Shaken, she swore she heard a voice in her head telling her to stop and help the animal, as it was a nice doggy.

The last time Ed had an encounter with one of these wolves was in July 2009. He was driving his car, his fiancée beside him in the passenger seat, when he saw a large, gray wolf sitting on the side of the highway. It got up and began following them until it moved ahead of them. It did this for an eighth of a mile before it disappeared by running faster.

They wondered if it finally tired of chasing the car when they saw it waiting on top of a sign in front of a church. What confounded them was the sign stood about 15 feet off the ground, and there was nothing the animal could have used to help it make it up to the top. Its eyes followed them as they drove past. Ed's girlfriend felt it speaking in her head until they had gotten far enough away to make it stop.

Next time you visit a deserted church or a bridge, or take that on-ramp, keep an eye out for its guardian. There might just be a dogman watching over it.

Dogman/Werewolf Stories That Ended Up on Travel Channel

"Not all monsters do monstrous things."
~Lydia Martin, "Teen Wolf"

Dogman Terror in North Carolina

Dave Leidy was driving slowly down a remote road in coastal North Carolina after one in the morning. He and his wife, Lisa, were looking for a safe spot to park their truck and trailer, so, they could camp for the night. They were startled by the sound of a loud bump against the rear of their Airstream, so Dave stopped and got out to investigate.

Moving to the back of his trailer, he noticed a large dent below the right taillight. He noticed the lack of insect noises and a strong sense of being hunted overcame him. He unholstered his .357 Magnum as the sense of dread increased. Movement of something in the marsh just off the road reached his ears. When he looked that way, his brain couldn't seem to process what he saw.

The moon shone down on a larger version of one of his German Shepherds. Then it did something that still haunts him. Dave heard two loud popping sounds as it reared up and stood on its hind legs.

The Dogman stared and growled at Dave before it looked to its right. Dave looked in the same direction. He saw another on all fours creeping toward him. It hit him that he was being flanked by the second dogman as the first held his attention. The first creature stepped forward and bared its teeth. Horrified, Dave saw both advancing on him.

Dave raised his pistol and fired. He felt sure he'd hit the first dogman in the shoulder. It stopped and Dave used the momentary pause to run to the driver's side of his truck, jump in, and hit the accelerator, roaring out of there. He looked in his side mirrors and counted two more coming up behind the first pair, also standing upright. All four gave chase until Dave neared 40 mph, then they slowed, peeled off the road, and head back into the marsh.

He kept driving and didn't stop until Lisa and he had made it to a town and spent the rest of the night in a well-lit parking lot.

Undeterred by that experience, I gather that Dave now investigates dogman sightings. He has had several more encounters of his own and told this story in the 5th episode of season one of the television series *Terror in the Woods* on *Travel Channel.*

Cajun Werewolf

I watched the *Monsters and Mysteries in America* episode on *Travel Channel* back in December 2020, as I saw it had a rougaru (loup garou) segment in this episode. One of those talking on it said the rougaru is cursed in this form for harm done to the swamp, and that these curses are very real.

Another, Neil Benson, went on about his own encounter with it as a 16-year-old teenager. He was paddling his boat through the swamp when he got the feeling someone or something was watching him. He was close to home when he saw it about 60 yards away. A creature or a man—he couldn't be sure what it was. He got away, but as his grownup self said, "It's easy for a man to hide in the swamp if he didn't want to be found, so it stands that something like that creature can exist there, too."

Another man, Beldron Forest, lives in Chauvin, Louisiana. The town has 3,000 people living in it and it is surrounded by swamp. He talked about how, as a 13-year-old kid, he went hunting one night and came across it in the swamp. He wasn't supposed to be out there.

His mother told him on All Souls Day and Saints Day, there are souls who walk the earth and so, he should never go hunting on those days. He brushed that off and went hunting on November 1, 1976. He noticed his dog didn't want to be out there.

The woods are full of squirrels, rabbits, and all sort of animals, but they saw nothing. He decided to go home when he saw a rabbit who froze. He pointed his gun at it.

Suddenly, something that looked doglike appeared, and it growled. Beldron bolted, kept running, feeling the heat on his back like it was close to him. Finally, he made it home and he no longer felt the heat. He'd learned his lesson, and never went hunting on All Souls Day again.

OTHER SHAPESHIFTERS

"Shapeshifting requires the ability to transcend your attachments, in particular your ego attachments to identity and who you are. If you can get over your attachment to labeling yourself and your cherishing of your identity, you can be virtually anybody. You can slip in and out of different shells, even different animal forms or deity forms."
~Zeena Schreck

Alaskan Shapeshifters

Each evening the night swallowed the sun and gave the raven the sun's energy. He stored this power in his wings, tinged with the blue of Alaskan skies."
~Suzy Davies

Werewolves and Dogmen are not the only shifters in the Last Frontier. There are the *Kushtaka* in both Tlingit and Tsimshian tales of southeastern Alaska. Then there are the shapeshifting beings in four Indigenous stories.

Some information about this state. Alaska was admitted to the Union as the 49th state on January 3, 1959. Its capital is Juneau. The name Alaska is derived from the Aleut word "Aleyska," meaning "great land."

Alaska lies at the extreme northwest of the North American continent, and the Alaska Peninsula is the largest peninsula in the Western Hemisphere. Because the 180th meridian passes through the state's Aleutian Islands, Alaska's westernmost portion is in the Eastern Hemisphere. Thus, technically, Alaska is in both hemispheres.

Alaska has an estimated 100,000 glaciers, ranging from tiny cirque glaciers to huge valley glaciers. Of the 20 highest peaks in the United States, 17 are in Alaska. Denali, the highest peak in North America, is 20,320 ft. above sea level. Denali, the Indigenous name for the peak, means "The Great One." The Yukon River, almost 2,000 miles long, is the third longest river in the U.S. There are more than 3,000 rivers in Alaska and over 3 million lakes.

There are more than 70 potentially active volcanoes in Alaska. Several have erupted in recent times. On March 27, 1964, North America's strongest recorded earthquake, with a moment magnitude of 9.2, rocked central Alaska. Each year, Alaska has approximately 5,000 earthquakes, including 1,000 that measure above 3.5 on the Richter scale. Of the 10 strongest earthquakes ever recorded in the world, three have occurred in Alaska.

There are bald eagles, black and brown bears, grizzlies, moose, caribou, wolves, otters, and many other animals and birds. There are also other cryptids and monsters, prehistoric mammoths, ghost stories, and UFOs connected to the state. Alaska sounds like both an interesting and scary state to explore.

Otter at the Richmond Metro Zoon in Mosley, Virginia

The Kushtaka (WereOtters) Alaska

Alaska is full of many legends and myths. It is the last frontier in the United States and way far north from the lower 48. Due to so much forest in the state, there are the expected numerous sasquatch sightings. Ghosts haunt many buildings and lands. There have been sea serpents and lake and river monsters seen. A dinosaur has been accounted in tales, too, and they even say mammoths are still alive in the Far North.

Witnesses have caught sight of Thunderbirds soaring the skies, cats impossible to believe in stalk the area, and people have encountered bears that are not the black, grizzly, or polar bear. Werewolves are said to prowl there, but they are not the only shapeshifter in lore about Alaska, for the state is also the land of the Kushtaka—or in English, the ottermen.

Some researchers claim they are just Bigfoot, but the Alaskan Indigenous tribes disagree. *Kushtaka* is in both Tlingit and Tsimshian tales of southeastern Alaska. Alternate spellings are *Kushtaka, Kooshdaa Kaa, Koushtaka,* and *Kooshdakhaa.*

They are shapeshifters able to take the form of an otter or a human. Most times, they are in-between—a half otter, half man bipedal. Standing between 6 and 8 feet tall and covered in sleek, black, or dark-brown fur, they have hands like a human, with sharp talons instead of fingernails. They walk on human feet, and their large eyes sometimes glow as some witnesses have described after encounters.

Needle sharp teeth crowd their mouths, and the beasts have a long tail. The sound they make is a high-pitched, three-part whistle that goes low-high-low. These beings have vast supernatural powers.

The stories claim they prey on children, taking human form or using the child's relatives' or friends' voices to lure them away.

Just like the skinwalkers, it is taboo to speak of them, as even to mention them is to attract their unwanted attention. So, many try to never say their name.

Historians believe that Tlingit mothers used the Kushtaka as a bogeyman to keep their little ones from disobeying the rules of the tribe. "Don't say their name or go alone into the woods, or the Kushtaka will steal you far away!"

Not just folklore, the First Nations people are serious about the ottermen. It is the same as the skinwalker is to the Navajo; the threat is real.

Strangely, the otter would be chosen as the shape to shift into because otters are playful and joyous animals, sociable and industrious. Not monstrous or evil things at all. And yet, to the tribes in Alaska, the dark, otherworldly Kushtaka, take this form.

Anthropologist Richard Baraazzuol points out a possible why in his study of Tlingit beliefs in *The Tlingit Land Otter Complex: Coherence in the Social and Shamanic Order*. His written words tell that although the sea otter brought the tribe the most in wealth from fur trading until the near extinction of the animals in the 19th century, it was the land otter that is almost human-like in their environment. This led to the perception that there was a symbolic bridge uniting animals and humans—that it could function well both on the land and in the water. All these Indigenous beliefs pointed to it representing an in-between being—one with supernatural powers.

One story told about one 4-year-old boy who didn't listen to his mother about venturi, a tree's roots, not wearing any clothes. Luckily for him, he pooped on himself, and the monsters didn't want to touch him after that.

Except the Indigenous tribes say, even if they survive capture by the Kushtaka, they are still never the same as before. Some go insane. Like the story of one girl recovered, but raged and attacked everyone, biting and punching anyone who tried to hold her, then ripping off her clothing to run around in her birthday suit.

Another encounter was related in an article in the *Petersburg Pilot*, dated May 19, 1994. A hunter from the Tlingit tribe was deep in the woods of the infamous "Devil's Country" of Thomas Bay. He paused when he heard a whistling sound. Once that stopped, he heard his name called out. A strange feeling overcame him, and he understood that it must be a Kushtaka, attempting to get him. Remembering what to do to free himself of the creature's magic, he snatched up a branch and bit into the wood. The feeling leaving him, he escaped from the area. After that, he never hunted again.

The Indigenous shaman is said to have the ability to travel between worlds, and because they can, they can save those taken by the Kushtaka and bring them back to everyday human existence. Kushtakas were once human beings in other worlds, transformed by land otters into creatures like themselves. The creatures were still able to maintain some human qualities. No longer truly human, they would kidnap children, scare women, and cause storms, avalanches, disease, and famine. Raven bestowed the dual-role gifts of living on both land and underwater to land otters, along with the powers of illusion and disguise. Raven also gave land otters a mission of saving those lost at sea and in the woods, and being able to shift into a half-otter, half-human beings.

The Kushtaka may have the ability to do good, and yet, they kill humans by their teeth and claws, ripping their victims apart into pieces. Meanwhile, they can also do good, saving those lost in the wilderness or from drowning.

But, there is one problem with being saved by a Kushtaka: it means being transformed into an otterman so the person can survive frigid temperatures or the freezing waters.

One becomes a Kushtaka because illusions of the human's family and friends appear, so they might be distracted while the change is happening. As the morphing goes on, the person becomes a hybrid creature, more otter than man. Although this is for their survival, it is more a curse than a saving grace, for they are forever trapped in this shape, unable to return home and never the same in mind.

The Tlingit people believe being made into one of the otter people is terrifying. For to be able to be reincarnated when they die and find peace, they must die human. Unless a shaman can bring the person back from this form, the shapeshifter is forever lost. Sometimes, if someone comes by while a person is being transformed and they recognize the other, they can be brought back from the brink of complete change. To the Tlingit, not finding someone who is lost or drowned is horrible. For them to change or die means the soul cannot reincarnate back into the clan's lineage. It means there is nobody to cremate and that the Kushtaka can take the drowned victim and make them into one of them.

Were the missing utterly lost at sea or due to blizzards on land, or had the Kushtaka took them? Because the otterman could take its victims deep into its dens along riverbanks, where enchanted, the man, woman, or child would believe they were at home, even eat of the food offer them there, until the transformation was complete. It is interesting to note that partaking of food from the Kushtaka is the same offered by fairies in European myths—eat of it, and you are forever stuck in their world.

Even more frightening about the Kushtaka than their ability to shapeshift is their ability to hypnotize and drive people insane. They can also mimic a child crying or a woman's screams. Not just children, but even hunters and those out in boats on the water, are in danger from these creatures.

The transformation is thought to go like this: hair grows over the body, then the speech becomes confused, the person begins to walk on his elbows and knees, a tail sprouts out from the behind, and slowly he becomes more otter than human. Upon seeing someone, if he is recognized, he can be saved, or if his drowned body is found, he can be cremated and saved that way.

Anyone saved from this is a proven candidate to become a shaman. Their knowledge of the ottermen and having been once a part of that magic, would enable them to counsel others about the Kushtaka.

Around the Copper River area, they are also called the "long-tail men." It is thought the stories about this originated around Copper River, but it isn't sure. These creatures live, or had lived, under banks of rivers, deep in the mud. Their lairs are accessible by caves and holes, all along the riverbanks. The most frightening thing about these long-tailed people was their preferred diet of human flesh!

Not as smart as humankind, they still had a tribal structure with leaders. Active mostly at night, they are never seen because they are artful at camouflaging themselves.

An interesting story I ran across had the actor Charlie Sheen telling the celebrity news website and show, *TMZ*, that he traveled with friends to Alaska in 2013 so that he could search for the Land Otter People. Of course, he never found the shifters, instead citing, "It obviously knew our group was far too skilled to be snowed in this fashion, so it stayed hidden like a sissy."

The Kushtaka is afraid of dogs, so the Tlingit people keep dogs for their own protection. The wereotter is also afraid of urine, copper, and fire.

A Reverend Arthur R. Wright, happened to be of mixed race, having Indigenous blood due to his Athabaskan mother. The man became a missionary for the church and spent time among his mother's people in Alaska. He reported something in the early 1900s about a battle between the long-tailed people and warriors of the First Nations in the Copper River region. This account was published in the *Cordova Daily News*, in its February 7th edition.

It had happened on his most recent trip to the Copper River region that he saw numerous holes in an embankment. When he asked about them, the Indigenous Peoples said they were the holes of the men with tails. They then told him the story of when the natives, lured by the plentiful caribou in the Selina River country, settled there and built a village.

When a dog with a fishtail in its mouth wandered into their village, it puzzled them how it got this, as no one had been fishing. They went to check it out, to find out where the fish came from. By evening, none of the searchers returned, and those in the village wondered what happened.

One of their best trackers was sent to find them. He came upon a rope made of grass stretched across a path. It hit him that this was a trap. Making his way carefully and quietly, he traveled the path until he saw some caves in the distance. He waited under cover until, finally, some men walked out of the cave. The problem was, they had tails that dragged on the ground! It appeared they use these tails as a form of locomotion, using them between their legs to push themselves forward.

Making sure he stayed downwind of them, just in case they could catch his scent, he noticed that they kicked a ball around on the ground.

Not a ball, but a human head—one that had belonged to one of the missing men!

The tracker took off for his village, where he reported how many of the tailed men, plus the number of cave openings, he had seen. The men and boys that gathered around him decided they would seal off the caves using fire and smoke and hopefully manage to kill the tail men inside. Then they went to do as they had decided to do, even though it was raining by the time they had arrived. Even with arrows flying at them, the Indigenous men kept the tail men inside by the fire. Eventually, there were no more arrows, and when the fire died down, they found the tail men dead.

In these modern times, there are still stories concerning the Kushtaka being seen or heard. There are accounts of these creatures around the city of Haines. That people have seen them around several spots on the outskirts of the city during broad daylight.

Even with modernization and college educations, there are still some of Indigenous blood who won't speak of these beings, carrying the fear that this will cause them to come to seek that person out.

One man told a story about how he and his brother, home on a visit, had encountered one of the ottermen when they went camping. After they had set up the tent and settled in, they made a campfire, and sat around it, talking. They began hearing a high-pitched whistling, high, then low, then high again, returning to low, just like in the stories about the Kushtaka.

The man began feeling lightheaded, and he and his brother worried as the whistling continued, along with rustling sounds that changed locations like whatever was making it was moving around their camp. They even saw it, trying to hide behind a tree.

Frightened and worried it might be trying to make them like it, they grabbed their stuff, tore down the tent, and bolted back for home. When they told their grandfather about what they had heard and seen, he told them that was one of them.

Funny thing, even though dangerous, it is forbidden to kill one of them because it might be a long-lost relative. Besides, killing one might incite a war with the Kushtaka. There is strong regard to just leave them alone.

Eskimo Myths and Legends with Shapeshifters
Alaska

The Kushtaka are not the only shapeshifting beings in Alaska. There were the Dogmen and

werewolf stories I mentioned in the earlier
Werewolf and Dogman chapters in this book,
but there are also other shapeshifters in four
Indigenous myths.

Kiv-i-ung and the Seal Boy

An old woman and her son lived in a hut.
The old woman did not have a husband to help
her and the boy. They were so poor that the
young boy's clothing was made of birds'
feathers, as she didn't know how to hunt except
to make snares, and the boy was too young to
harpoon seals in the sea. Other children made
fun of the boy, calling him "Bird Boy." They
would call out, "Fly away, birdie!" The grownup men would grab at him and tear his clothes.
The only man who never did any of this was Kiv-
i-ung.

This angered the woman, and because she
knew how to do magic (this puzzled me as, if
she could do what she did to the boy next, why
couldn't she make clothes with her powers?),
she poured water on the mud floor, making a
puddle, and told him to step in it. When he did,
he sank into it and found himself as a seal on a
beach. Excited, the seal boy jumped into the sea
and began swimming around.

Because someone saw him, the men of the village grabbed their kayaks and began to head through the water toward him. The seal boy swam farther and farther out to sea, but the men followed him. He dove down under the water, coming up by their kayaks, luring them to keep pursuing him, just as his grandmother had bidden him do.

Far from the nearest land, suddenly, a great gale arose, causing the ocean to foam and roar. The water upended all the kayaks, and all the men drowned. Well, all but one.

Kiv-i-ung's kayak never capsized, but as he worked hard paddling, he kept drifting farther and farther away, just not back to where his village was. A dense fog rose, and he couldn't see which way to go but kept rowing for days.

One day, he saw some mass through the heavy mist and headed toward it. Luckily, he realized in time that this was a whirlpool, and he worked hard at staying away. When the fog lifted, he saw real land this time, and raced toward it, landing upon it where the first of his many adventures began, lasting until many years later. Like Rip Van Winkle, he found his village and was able to finally return home.

The Goose Wife

Because he could not get a young woman to marry him, Itajung left his village and traveled until he came to the land of the birds. The birds were all in the sea, their boots left on the land, so he grabbed one pair and hid with them.

The birds came out of the water and all, but one, a female goose, pulled on their boots. Itajung sprang out at her, and she saw he had her boots. The others flew off in fear of the human stranger. But the goose couldn't leave without hers.

Itajung said, "I will give you your boots if you become my wife."

The goose agreed, and he handed her the boots. She slipped them on and changed into a beautiful young woman. One who was more beautiful than those back at his village.

They wandered until they finally settled down in a village by the sea, as she liked to be near the water. She and Itajung lived there for many years, and the village was happy as he proved to be a good whaler.

One day, as he and the other villagers were cleaning and cutting the whale he'd caught, Itajung told his wife to come to help them as she sat not doing anything but watching.

She said, "I will not, for I will soil my nice white clothing." Once again, he told her to help. She replied, "I only eat the food of the land and never from the sea."

Upset with her, Itajung stood and had only taken a couple of steps when she snatched their son's hand, and both turned into geese and flew away.

Itajung searched for them and one day came upon a man called Small Salmon who was chopping wood with an ax. Itajung asked Small Salmon if he'd seen his wife and son. Small Salmon said he saw them on a small island in a large lake nearby, and that she had a new husband. This worried Itajung as he could not swim and had no way to get across the lake to the island.

But Small Salmon solved that by providing him with the backbone of a salmon that turned into a kayak, and Itajung used it to cross the waters to the shore of the island.

He walked toward a hut where he saw his son playing outside. His son saw him and ran indoors to tell his mother that his father was approaching.

His Mother said, "Go back to playing. Father is far away and cannot find us."

The boy did but saw that Itajung had drawn closer, and he ran back inside, saying. "Mother, Father is here and is coming to our hut."

"Go back outside to play. Father is far away and cannot find us."

He went out but came back in. "Father is here."

Itajung walked through the doorway. When the woman's new husband saw him, he said, "Open that box in the corner."

The woman did, and many feathers flew out of it and latched onto her, the man, and the small boy. All three became geese and flew away before Itajung could stop them.

Origin of the Narwhal

A young boy who hunted for food for his mother, his sister, and himself became blind one day as he never wore snow goggles outside. When he managed to find his way home, instead of being sad about what happened to her son, his mother became angry. She began ill-treating him, and even when he managed to shoot an arrow through a window and kill a polar bear, his mother and sister skinned and buried the meat in the snow, not telling him. She never gave him any of the meat, using it only to feed his sister and herself, and she made sure the sister never told him.

One day, a loon flew over the hut and saw that the boy was blind. The bird wanted to help him, so it bade the boy follow it to the ocean and took him on its back to dive down into the water. Each time the loon would bring the boy back up to the surface and ask if he could see. The boy said no, so down both would go again.

Finally, the boy could see and thanked the loon, who made him promise to never shoot another bird ever again.

The boy agreed.

The loon said, "Now, you can go home."

The boy found the furry skin of the bear hanging over the doorway, and he barged inside, demanding his mother tell him where the bearskin came from. He knew it came from the bear he'd shot, but he wanted her to admit it.

Instead, she told him, "Come here and eat what I made."

The boy didn't and again, demanded where she got the bearskin.

She told him some men in a boat came and gave it to her. Then, she told him to eat the food she'd made.

But the boy left the hut and went to the only other Inuit in the village and learned to make a harpoon. He went with him and others to hunt the white whales. Not having a kayak, he would tie a string around his waist and dive into the water to spear his own whales. Sometimes, his sister helped him.

Still angry at his mother, he got her to come one time and tied a string around her, telling her to go in the water so he could spear a whale. She cried for him to do a dolphin instead, but he told her those were too big and heavy.

When he saw a whale, he yelled, "There is one!" He pushed her into the water and threw his spear, hitting the animal, but only wounding it.

He called out to his mother, "This is because you abused me."

The whale dragged her out to sea, where she transformed into a narwhal.

Bird Shifters

The Indigenous Peoples from the northern edge of Puget Sound to along the coast to the Bering Strait believe that the eagle, the raven, the goose, and any other bird, can push up its beak like a cap and become a man, and push down the beak, and turn back into a bird again. Many stories of the Inuit have Raven able to push up his beak and become a man, and help make people and animals. In one tale, he got a wife, who was a goose who pushed her beak up and became a woman. Eventually, a story had some ravens lose their magic and stay ordinary ravens.

Shapeshifting Witches

Are you a good witch, or a bad witch?
~Wizard of Oz

Witches, sorcerers, and wizards around the world have used magic to transform into other forms. The witches in this chapter are connected to Indigenous and Hispanic people, but the last witch is from Massachusetts, the state famous for the Salem witch trials.

Skinwalkers in the American Southwest

Werewolves, Ottermen, other shifters, or dogmen are not the only such creatures stalking in the United States; there are others, too. One such being is the skinwalker.

In the American Southwest, the Navajo, Hopi, Utes, and some other tribes each have their own version of the skinwalker story, but they all end up to the same thing—a malevolent witch capable of transforming itself into a wolf, coyote, bear, bird, or other animal. In other words, by using black magic.

The witch might wear the hide or skin of the animal identity he/she wants to assume, and when the transformation is complete, the human witch inherits the speed, strength, or cunning of the animal whose shape it has taken. Sometimes, it even completely becomes the animal, as people claim to see a coyote or bird running off into the desert or canyons after they were attacked by a skinwalker before it takes off.

Skinwalkers avoid the light and their eyes glow like an animal's when in their human body, but when they assume an animal form, their eyes do not glow as an animal's would do.

In the Navajo language, yee naaldlooshii translates to "by means of it, it goes on all fours." The yee naaldlooshii is one of several varieties of, specifically, a type of 'ánti'įhnii.' The legend of the skinwalkers is not well understood outside of the Navajo culture, mostly due to reluctance to discuss the subject with outsiders. Navajo people are reluctant to reveal skinwalker lore to non-Navajos, or to discuss it at all among those they do not trust. After all, a stranger who asks questions about skinwalkers just might be one himself, looking for his next victim.

To gain the 'ánti'įhnii status, often a greedy person who wants to become a skinwalker will do many horrible things—such as even murder someone in their own family. Navajo witches, including skinwalkers, represent the antithesis of Navajo cultural values. While community healers and cultural workers are known as medicine men and women, or by terms in the local, Indigenous language, witches are seen as evil, performing twisted ceremonies and manipulating magic in a perversion of the medicine of the good work people traditionally perform.

To practice their good works, traditional healers learn about both good and evil magic. Most can handle the responsibility, but some people can become corrupt and choose to become witches. Once they become this evil entity, they will make people ill and even commit murders. They are grave robbers and necrophiliacs.

Practitioners of witchcraft are believed to be real in the Navajo community, and few Navajo want to cross paths with the yee naaldlooshii, or what we call the skinwalkers. They will not speak of these beings, especially with strangers, as doing so might attract the attention of one and bring it to where they are. These beings practice a form of witchery that is connected to corpses and death. Navajos try to avoid death. To the Navajo and other tribes of the southwest, the tales of skinwalkers are not a mere legend.

The four basic ways of the skinwalker include witchery, sorcery, wizardry, and frenzy. These are simply additional parts of the Navajo people. The Navajo believe people must live in harmony with the earth. They believe that there are two classes of people: Earth people, meaning mortals, and those who are Holy People, unseen spiritual beings.

Animals associated with witchcraft include tricksters, such as the coyote, but may also include other creatures, such as the crow, wolf, owl, or fox—usually those associated with death or bad omens. It is said that they can assume the form of any animal. Skinwalkers might also possess living animals or people, then walk around in their bodies after locking eyes with them. They may be male or female.

Because skinwalkers use the forms of a carnivore, it is forbidden to wear any furs or feathers from these animals. Sheep and calfskin are acceptable.

Dine' believe that skinwalkers use spit, hair, and nail clippings to curse their victims. This is why many Navajo never spit on the ground or even leave their shoes outside the door, and they make sure all nail and hair clippings are disposed of properly or burned.

In the legends, it is said the yee naaldlooshii curse people and cause great suffering and death. At night, their eyes glow red like hot coals. It is said that if you see the face of one of them, they will have to kill you because if you know who they are, they will die. If you see one, and even if you do not know the creature's human form, they must kill you to keep you from finding out who they are.

They use a mixture of what some call corpse powder, that they make from flesh and bones of the dead, which they blow into your face. Your tongue turns black, and you go into convulsions and eventually die. They also make corpse beads from the dead, as well. They shoot these into their intended victims. They are known to use evil spirits in their ceremonies.

The Dine' have learned ways to protect themselves against this evil, always keeping on guard. It is even said besides animal shapes, they may steal a human being's skin and shift to look like that person.

Raps around your home are attributed by some Dine' as caused by a skinwalker trying to get your attention.

There is a difference of opinion among the Dine' that other races outside of Indigenous Peoples can be cursed or affected. Some believe not, while others feel anyone can if they believe in the possibility.

The Southwest region is where these shapeshifting witches live, stretching from the Mojave Desert in California to Carlsbad, New Mexico, and from the Mexico–United States border to the southern areas of Colorado, Utah, and Nevada. The largest metropolitan areas are centered around Phoenix, Las Vegas, Tucson, Albuquerque, and El Paso. Those five metropolitan areas have an estimated total population of more than 9.6 million as of 2017, with nearly 60 percent of them living in the two Arizona cities—Phoenix and Tucson.

Human history in the Southwest begins with the arrival of the Clovis culture, a Paleo-Indian hunter-gatherer culture that arrived sometime around 9000 BC. This culture remained in the area for several millennia. At some point, they were replaced by three great Pre-Columbian cultures: The Ancestral Pueblo people, the Hohokam people, and the Mogollon people, all of whom existed among other surrounding cultures, including the Fremont and Patayan. Maize began to be cultivated in the region sometime during the early first millennium BC, but it took several hundred years for the Indigenous cultures to be dependent on it as a food source. Around 1500, as their dependence on maize grew, Pre-Columbian peoples began developing irrigation systems.

According to archeological finds, the Ancestral Pueblo people, also known as the Anasazi (although that term is becoming more and more disused), began settling in the area in approximately 1500 BC. They would spread throughout the entire northern section of the Southwest. This culture would go through several different eras, lasting from approximately 1500 BC through the middle of the 15th century AD. As the Puebloans transitioned from a nomadic lifestyle to one based on agriculture, their first domiciles were pithouses.

The Mogollon culture developed later than the Puebloan, arising in the eastern area of the region at around 300 BC. Their range would eventually extend deep into what would become Mexico and dominate the southeastern portion of the Southwest. Their settlements would evolve over time from pit-dwellings through pueblos and finally also incorporating cliff-dwellings.

The Hohokam were the last of these ancestral cultures to develop, somewhere around AD 1, but they would grow to be the most populous of the three by AD 1300, despite being the smallest of the three in terms of area, covering most of the southwest portion. Beginning in approximately AD 600, the Hohokam began to develop an extensive series of irrigation canals. Of the three major cultures in the Southwest, only the Hohokam developed irrigation as a means of watering their agriculture.

Not long after the Hohokam reached the height of their culture, all three major cultures in the Southwest began to decline, for unknown reasons, although severe drought and encroachment from other peoples have been postulated. By the end of the 15th century, all three cultures had disappeared. The modern Indigenous tribes of the Hopi, Zuni, Acoma, and Laguna trace their ancestry back to the ancestral Puebloans, while the Akimel O'odham and Tohono O'odham claim descent from Hohokam. The area previously occupied by the Mogollon was taken over by an unrelated tribe, the Apache. While it is unclear whether any of the modern Indigenous tribes are descended from the Mogollon, some archeologists and historians believe that they mixed with Ancestral Puebloans and became part of the Hopi and Zuni.

Prior to the arrival of Europeans, what is now the Southwestern United States was inhabited by an exceptionally large population of Indigenous tribes. The area once occupied by the ancestral Puebloans became inhabited by several other tribes, the most populous of which were the Navajo, Ute, Southern Paiute, and Hopi.

The Navajo, along with the Hopi, were the earliest of the modern Indigenous tribes to develop in the Southwest. Around AD 1100, their culture began to develop in the Four Corners area of the region. The Ute could be found over most of modern-day Utah and Colorado, as well as northern New Mexico and Arizona. The Paiutes roamed an area that covered over 45,000 square miles of southern Nevada and California, south-central Utah, and northern Arizona. The Hopi settled the lands of the central and western portions of northern Arizona. Their village of Oraibi settled in approximately AD 1100 and is one of the oldest continuously occupied settlements in the United States. The Mogollon area became occupied by the Apaches and the Zuni. The Apache migrated into what is now the American Southwest from the northern areas of North America at some point between 1200 and 1500. They settled throughout New Mexico, eastern Arizona, northern Mexico, parts of western Texas, and southern Colorado. The Zuni count their direct ancestry through the ancestral Puebloans. The modern-day Zuni established a culture along the Zuni River in far-eastern Arizona and western New Mexico. Both major tribes of the O'odham settled in the southern and central Arizona, in the lands once controlled by their ancestors, the Hohokam.

The first Europeans were Spanish. The first intrusion into the region from them came from the south. In 1539, a Jesuit Franciscan named Marcos de Niza led an expedition from Mexico City, passing through eastern Arizona. The following year, Francisco Vázquez de Coronado, based on reports from survivors of the Narváez expedition (1528–36), who crossed eastern Texas on their way to Mexico City, led an expedition to discover the Seven Golden Cities of Cibola.

Antonio de Espejo's expedition in 1582-1583 explored what is now New Mexico and eastern Arizona, and led to Juan de Oñate's establishment of the Spanish province of Santa

Fe de Nuevo México in 1598, with a capital founded near Ohkay Owingeh Pueblo, which he called San Juan de Los Caballeros. Oñate's party also attempted to establish a settlement in what is now Arizona in 1599, but they were turned back by inclement weather. In 1610, Santa Fe was founded, making it the oldest capital in the United States.

It was when the United States. began its expansion, and other Europeans, not just the Spanish, and Americans, began settling the Southwest as much as elsewhere. Eventually, when many of these territories became states and the Navajo, Zuni, Apache, Ute, and Southern Paiute were forced onto reservations, with the Navajo having the largest. And so, their legends and myths stayed with the Indigenous tribes, including those of the skinwalker.

Skinwalker stories told among Navajo children may be complete life and death struggles that end in either skinwalker or Navajo killing the other, or partial encounter stories that end in a stalemate. Navajo victory stories are composed as encounter tales, with the evil creature approaching a hogan or house and being scared away.

Non-Indigenous interpretations of these skinwalker stories take the form of partial encounter stories on the road, where the protagonist is temporarily vulnerable but then escapes from the skinwalker in a way not traditionally seen in Navajo stories that take place away from home.

These beings use mind control, making their victims hurt themselves and ending their lives. They are considered powerful, able to run faster than a car, no matter how the driver speeds up, and can jump mesa cliffs without any effort.

A Nevada attorney, Michael Stuhff, is one of the few lawyers in the history of American jurisprudence who filed legal papers against a Navajo witch.

As a young attorney in the mid-1970s, Stuhff worked in a legal aid program based near Ganado, Arizona, with many of his clients being Navajo. He confronted a witch in a dispute over child custody.

His client was a Navajo woman who lived on the reservation with her son. She wanted full custody rights and back child support payments from her estranged husband, an Apache man. At one point, the husband got permission to take the son out for an evening, but he didn't return the boy until the next day. The son later told his mother what had happened.

He had spent the night with his father and a "medicine man." They built a fire atop a cliff and, for many hours, the medicine man performed ceremonies, songs, and incantations around the fire. At dawn, they went to some woods by a cemetery and dug a hole. The medicine man placed two dolls in the hole, one was dark and the other made of light wood, both meant to be the mother and her lawyer. Stuhff didn't know how to approach this, so he consulted a Navajo professor at a nearby community college.

The professor told him it sounded like a powerful and serious type of ceremony, meant for the lawyer to end up buried in the graveyard for real. He also said a witch could perform this type of ceremony only four times in his or her life because if tried more than that, the curse will come back on the witch themself. If the intended victim discovered it, then the curse would come back onto the person who requested it.

Stuhff filed court papers that requested an injunction against the husband and the unknown medicine man, whom he described in the court documents as "John Doe, A Witch," to let the husband know he knew what he and the witch had done. He described the alleged ceremony in detail.

This upset the opposing attorney by the motion, as were the husband and the presiding judge. The opposing lawyer argued to the court that the medicine man had performed "a blessing way ceremony," not a curse. But Stuhff knew that the judge, who was a Navajo, would be able to distinguish between a blessing ceremony, which takes place in Navajo hogans, and a darker ceremony involving lookalike dolls that took place in the woods near a cemetery, which he did.

Before the judge ruled, though, Stuhff requested a recess so that the significance of his legal motion could sink in. The next day, the husband agreed to grant total custody to the mother and pay all back child support.

Whether or not Stuhff believed that witches have supernatural powers, he acknowledged the Navajos did. Specific communities on the reservation had reputations as witchcraft strongholds, and the lawyer wasn't confident that the witch he faced was a skinwalker or not.

"Not all witches are skinwalkers," he said, "but all skinwalkers are witches.

Skinwalkers are at the top of the food chain, a witch's witch, purely evil in intent. They possess knowledge of medicine, both practical medicine (heal the sick) and spiritual (maintain harmony).

The flip side of the skinwalker coin is the power of tribal medicine men. Among the Navajo, medicine men train many years to become full-fledged practitioners in the mystical rituals of the Dine' (Navajo) people. The word Dine' is from their language and means "the people." "Navajo" comes from a Tewa-Puebloan, word "nava hu" meaning "place of large, planted fields."

Except there's a dark side to the learning of the medicine men. Witches follow some of the same training and obtain similar knowledge as their more benevolent colleagues, but they supplement this with their pursuit of the dark arts. By Navajo law, a known witch has forfeited its status as a human and can be killed at will.

Witchcraft was always an accepted, if not widely acknowledged, part of Navajo culture. The killing of witches was historically accepted among the Navajo, as it had been among the Europeans. In the Navajo Witch Purge of 1878, more than 40 Navajo witches were killed, "purged" by tribe members. The Navajo endured a horrendous forced march at the U.S. Army's hands. Hundreds were starved, murdered, or left to die before the survivors were confined to a bleak reservation, leaving them destitute and starving.

The Navajo assumed that witches might be responsible for their plight, so they retaliated by purging their ranks of any suspected witches. Tribe members reportedly found a collection of witch artifacts wrapped in a copy of the Treaty of 1868 and "buried in the belly of a dead person."

Although skinwalkers are believed to prey only on Indigenous Peoples, recent reports from non-Indigenous Peoples claim they had encountered skinwalkers while driving on or near tribal lands.

One New Mexico Highway Patrol officer had his own experience while patrolling a highway south of Gallup, New Mexico. He had had two separate encounters with a ghastly creature that seemingly attached itself to the door of his vehicle. During the first encounter, the veteran law enforcement officer said the unearthly being appeared to be wearing a ghostly mask and costume as it kept pace with his patrol car. To his horror, he realized that the person wasn't attached to his door after all. Instead, it ran alongside his vehicle as he roared at a high rate of speed down the highway.

The officer said he had a nearly identical experience in the same area a few days later. He was shaken to his core by these encounters but didn't realize that he would soon get confirmation that what he had seen was real. While having coffee with a fellow highway patrolman, not long after the second incident, the cop cautiously described his two experiences. To his amazement, the second officer admitted to having his own encounter with a white-masked ghoul, a being that appeared out of nowhere and managed to keep pace with his cruiser as he raced across the desert.

The first officer still patrols the same stretch of highway but is petrified every time he passes that particular spot.

A Caucasian family still speaks in hushed tones about their encounter with a skinwalker, even though it happened back in 1983. One night, they were driving along Route 163 through the Navajo Reservation, when suddenly the family got this weird feeling that someone was following them. As the father slowed down the truck as they came to a sharp bend, the atmosphere changed, and time itself seemed to slow down when something suddenly leaped out of a ditch.

"It was black and hairy and appeared eye level with the cab," one of the family members recalled. "Whatever this thing was, it wore a man's white and blue checked shirt and long pants. Its arms were raised over its head, almost touching the top of the cab. It looked like a hairy man or an animal. But it didn't look like an ape or anything like that. It had yellow eyes, and it had its mouth open wide."

The father served two tours in Vietnam, and nothing had scared him during the war, but his wife said he looked completely pale, as if the blood had drained from his face. The father admitted being scared as goosebumps erupted from his skin. Although time seemed frozen during this bizarre interlude, he kept driving until the family was soon miles down the highway.

Days later, the family awoke to the sounds of loud drumming at their home in Flagstaff. Everyone bolted to the front room and peered out the windows and saw the dark forms of three men outside their fence, trying to climb it to enter the yard and inexplicably appeared unable to cross onto the property. Frustrated by their failed entry, the men chanted as the terrified family huddled inside the house. The strangest thing about this was if these were skinwalkers, why didn't they assume birds' shapes and fly over the fence?

The family didn't call the police. Instead, a family member called a Navajo friend. During the daytime, the woman came out and walked through the house and told them it had been skinwalkers, that the intrusion failed because something protected the family. She admitted that it was all highly unusual since skinwalkers rarely bother the non-Indigenous but performed a blessing ceremony anyway. Nothing disturbed the family after that, and they never drove that stretch of road again.

There is a ranch in Utah called Skinwalker Ranch because there have been so many skinwalker sightings besides UFOs and even spirits haunting. Skinwalker Ranch—also known as the Sherman or Gorman Ranch—occupies around 480 acres in Uintah County, Utah and is beset by paranormal activity.

The property borders the Ute Indian Reservation, and its eerie reputation dates back to native folklore. Amongst the tribe, there's a belief that the area has been tormented for hundreds of years by skinwalkers. To the Utes, the site is cursed, known as the "path of the skinwalker."

Terry and Gwen Sherman purchased the property in 1994 with hopes of establishing a cattle ranch. The couple's first encounter with the paranormal came when they moved their furniture into their new home. As they worked, a large wolf appeared in a nearby cow pasture. The animal seemed strangely untroubled by the Shermans' presence. Suddenly, the wolf attacked the cattle and snatched a calf, biting into its leg.

Terry grabbed his rifle and shot the animal at close range. The wolf still stood. Terry reshot it, and again, the animal appeared unhurt. It merely trotted away. When Terry checked the ground, he didn't find any traces of blood. He tracked in the direction where the animal went off, but he didn't find any prints or blood.

For the Shermans, this was merely the beginning of their strange experiences at Skinwalker Ranch. The family would find crop circles scorched into the ground near their home; groceries mysteriously repacked and reorganized throughout their kitchen; once, after a set of bulls went missing, Terry discovered the animals crammed into a disused trailer in a seemingly hypnotized state. Another time, Terry saw what he believed to be an RV pull into the driveway, but when he approached it, the vehicle lifted into the air and flew away.

Each family member had trouble sleeping and, when they did sleep, were troubled by nightmares. In the morning, the Shermans awoke and discussed their identical dreams. They began sleeping together in the main room of the house.

Disembodied voices chattered at the family in strange languages. Cows repeatedly vanished, only to turn up killed and mutilated. After chasing a floating orb of light, a trio of ranch dogs disappeared into the night, and the family never found them again.

Then the Shermans were offered a deal they were only too happy to accept. In 1996, they left the property for good, handing over the keys and deed to the person who bought it from them, Robert Bigelow, founder of the National Institute for Discovery Science (NIDSci), a privately funded (and now defunct) research organization of ufology and the paranormal.

A young man lived in the rural, southern part of Nevada, towards the edge of town close to the open desert. It was late, somewhere between midnight and 2:00 a.m.

His friend had come over to spend the night hanging out. They sat in the living room, right next to a couple of closed windows that both had blinds hanging over them. Somehow, both got on the paranormal topic when the discussion led to the Navajo and Southern Paiute skinwalker lore. They had been talking an hour about skinwalkers when a faint, but unmistakable pitter-patter caught their attention outside the window. It sounded like something pacing back and forth the length of the side of the house. It went quiet when they stopped talking, so they thought maybe they hadn't heard anything. Then, all of a sudden, a loud hyena-like cackling erupted from outside.

Knowing that no wild animal they knew made sounds like that and scared, they wondered if they had attracted a real skinwalker by speaking about them, as that is a staple of the lore. Thinking that maybe it might be prudent not to acknowledge they heard it, they continued their conversation until they didn't hear anything else. At least, they hoped it had left.

Neither one felt willing to open the blinds or go outside to check, not until the morning. When both men woke up, they stepped out and found tracks of a dog, as large as their shoes in the dirt beneath the windows. The prints headed to the carport and, from there, to the yard's center before they vanished.

To this day, both men are positive that a skinwalker had visited that night. To their relief, it never returned, and the one man assumed that maybe it felt it had scared them enough. He admitted they never talked about skinwalkers after that night in his home ever again.

One woman of Navajo blood (I will use the name, Jenny—not her real name) had moved out east after a failed marriage to pursue a fashion design career, which went well for her. Although Jenny was still in contact with her sister (who I will call Lisa) on the Navajo reservation, she had never been back until Lisa contacted her that their mother had passed away.

Jenny flew back home and, there alone with her sister in their mother's home, Lisa told her a strange story about their mother and a man she had been seeing, plus a peculiar group of friends that Mom and her "boyfriend" hung out with.

The mother was on the verge of death when she made the sister listen to something to get it off her chest and die in peace. She told Lisa that the man and their friends were skinwalkers. Lisa knew that her mother was spending time with people who acted like witches because she had followed her mother and the man to a spot out in the desert at night, where the man wore nothing more than what looked like coyote or wolf skins and danced and chanted. Afterward, everyone began drinking alcohol, and Lisa left as her mother started getting "sickeningly" drunk, as she called it.

Their mother went on to tell her that skinwalkers can curse someone to death, and the man did just that with the next-door neighbor Mom had been taking care of when she became suddenly ill. Eventually, the neighbor died, and supposedly a will was left, leaving the house and the woman's belongings to Lisa's and Jenny's mother. Their mother went to the courthouse to fill out the appropriate papers when to her surprise, a young woman came in, saying she was the dead woman's daughter. Their mother never knew there was a daughter, but the young woman had proof, and so their mother couldn't get the house. That was when a falling out between the mother and the man came to be.

Jenny assisted her sister in getting things done and their parent buried, besides investigating her mother's claims. Those of the tribe told her to forget what her mother told her, for hers and her sister's sake. She let her sister have the house and went back to New York. Jenny felt sure many were relieved, and although she hasn't been around since, she still stays in communication with her sister.

Interestingly enough, there is a murder court case connected to a skinwalker. Navajo nurse Mary Saganitso, who worked at the Flagstaff Medical Center in Flagstaff, New Mexico, was found raped and strangled to death on a rocky slope behind the center in 1986, one of her nipples bitten off. This was the first murder in almost two decades.

George Abney, who had taught at Northern Arizona University at one time, admitted to the murder. Dental impressions proved to the prosecution that it was his bite marks that took off her nipple.

The accused murderer's defending team of Aspey, Watkins, and Diesel tried to prove that a skinwalker did the murder. Their witnesses included an Apache sweat lodge leader and a folklore professor married to a Navajo and who lived on the reservation.

Significant amounts of flesh and fatty tissue from Saganitso's body, the presence of "grass" near the murder site, and a stick lain carefully across the corpse were crucial elements in the case. Although many did believe Abney committed the murder, the jury decreed otherwise. Abney was acquitted.

The next time you vacation in New Mexico, or even Arizona, and decide to take a drive near or on reservation lands, keep an eye out for coyotes or deer rushing out of the brush and across the road and don't hit them. It may not be a real animal, but some evil witch, out looking to cause some mischief or curse unwary travelers.

La Lechuza as Owls (Public Domain)

Owl Witches
(La Lechuza, Tah-tah-kle'-ah, and Stikini)
New Mexico, Texas, and Washington

Humans changing shapes like werewolves or skinwalkers are not the only kinds of shapeshifters or witches. There is also La Lechuza.

La Lechuza means "the owl" in Spanish. But local stories called it the Owl Witch. Mayans believed that once the sun went down, the owls who were guardians of the dead came out. This shapeshifting witch is seen mainly in the Southwest, but it can be anywhere else in the United States, primarily due to the growing Hispanic population. They love to eat humans, especially children, who were said to be exceptionally flavorful.

The tale goes that a woman practiced black magic. The locals found out, and they burned her to death. But to their horror, she came back to life. She looked like a woman dressed in black during the day, but at night, she shifted to a human-sized owl with a human face, looking for revenge.

She searches during the night for prey, drawing them to her by whistling or wailing like a baby. When a foolish human investigates, La

Lechuza grabs them and flies off with them to their death.

The owl itself is a symbol of death in many Indigenous cultures. What's remarkable about La Lechuza is how widespread the legend is. The tribes of what is now northern Mexico were relatively isolated from one another, yet they each have their own story of these creepy owl-witches.

People would claim giant raven-black birds followed them at night, and the next morning they would find scratches on their doors or around windows. In one tale, a couple suspected their next-door elderly neighbor of being a witch, but they didn't have any proof. So, one night when the couple saw a large black bird flying around their home, the husband snatched his gun and shot at it. The bird screeched and flew away. They kept watch on the old woman's house, but she didn't appear outside of the place for several days. When she did, she walked out of the house with a pronounced limp.

In the 10th episode of Season 2 of *Monsters and Mysteries in America on the Travel Channel*, they had a portion of the hour about a La Lechuza. I watched it in 2020, but it originally aired in February 2014.

One man, Octavio Ramos, was a tech writer whose parents came from Mexico. When he and his wife had a baby, they moved into a house in Roswell, New Mexico, in the fall of 1964. It was rent free, long as they took care of it and the land.

Ramos had to water the landscape and plants, and was in charge of the generator, making sure it kept working. He checked the generator the last thing every day, meaning it was just before dusk. When he did this, he saw a fireball rising from his neighbor's home and a few came their way. This phenomenon happened every night, causing their dogs to bark before they broke into howling in fear.

Finally, Ramos felt brave enough to go outdoors in the dark and walked over to the barn, where he found owls in the hayloft. He ran back and told his wife. They heard something walking on their roof and down the side of their house, not in the light footsteps of an owl, but something big and bulky,

His wife contacted a good witch the next day. The woman told them what to do, as both he and his baby were in danger from the owl witch.

He took a crucifix and willed the owl witch to manifest into the fireball. When it did, he shot at it. It vanished, and only a few feathers and blood fell to the ground. He wasn't sure he killed the owl witch, but it never came back to torment him and his family again.

Another story concerns an owl witch and two teenagers from Austin, Texas. David Garcia and Mike Andreas decided to check out an abandoned building. The air inside felt chilly, but when they saw "things" scuttling around, and items fell; both boys heard a woman talking in a place where they were the only living beings around.

The boys went to check out what had fallen when something screeched, and a large, dark bird of some kind flew over them to a window. They bolted from the building where they saw no bird but a young girl with eyes that appeared as dark chasms staring at them.

Tah-tah-kle-ah—Yakima Washington

The Yakama tribe of Washington state have a remarkably similar legend like La Lechuza. It is a creature called the Tah-tah-kle'-ah.

These five supernatural women resemble giant owls, dwelling in caves by day and flying out at night to prey on all manner of animals—

including humans. They are said to prefer the taste of children. Legend has it they can hunt humans by mimicking their language.

Stikini—Seminole
Florida

The Stikini are sinister monsters from Seminole folklore. They are also known as the Man-Owls. These, like the two other owl shifters, are evil witches who transformed themselves into owl-beings. By day they still resemble Seminole people, but by night, they vomit up their souls (along with all their internal organs) and become undead owl-monsters that feed on human hearts.

In some Seminole communities, speaking their name is thought to put you at risk for turning into one, so Stikini stories are only told by certain medicine people. (Again, like with other Indigenous shapeshifters, don't speak of them, or they might come to you.) In other communities, they have been spoken of more casually as bogeymen to frighten children.

The Stikini looked like other Seminole people during the day, but when it became night, they changed completely. Not unlike a vampire turning into a bat in fiction, the Stikini used a more werewolf-like transformation. Once the moon rose, they would vomit up their souls, internal organs, and blood, transforming into undead owl-monsters that feasted upon human flesh.

I couldn't find out if the change was purposeful or forced by the rising moon. The witches travel deep into the woods to shift, keeping away from prying eyes. After it was done, they hung their internal organs high in the trees to prevent wild animals from eating them, so that by dawn, they could get their humanness back. This transformation represented the spiritual being of the Stikini and the "human" appearance it wears during the day is nothing more than a mask.

The owl-humanoids have tremendous strength and power, and can rip a grown man in two with ease. The word itself is so powerful that among some Seminoles, the belief of merely speaking Stikini aloud would attract one to them, or they would risk becoming one. Often, Stikini lore was only spoken aloud by powerful medicine men and women in the community, as only they could protect themselves against these hateful creatures.

In addition to their habit of eating hearts, the Stikini also take on a banshee-like role. The cry of one of them is very guttural and horrible, and if anyone hears the sound, it is said to be an omen of coming death.

There are some ways to protect yourself against a Stikini. For example, if you fear a Stikini is using your town as hunting grounds, try to find where they hung their organs. Destroy those, and the Stikini can't return to its human form. Like vampires and other creatures of the night, they can also be killed or grievously harmed by direct sunlight, as they cannot retreat to their human form.

In 1835, the United States moved forward with plans to relocate all the Seminole west of the Mississippi. When a small group of elderly Seminole women living along the Hillsborough River, north of Fort Brooke, heard, they became enraged and refused to move, raising a threat that Fort Brooke would be forever cursed.

It didn't matter, as over a hundred soldiers left Fort Brooke heading northward. The first morning after the soldiers set up camp, a young soldier was found dead. An investigation concluded that the man's heart had been removed. This same scenario happened night after night.

Remembering the Seminole womens' curse, soldier Joseph Sprague abandoned his post. As he fled through the forest at dusk, he saw a group of Seminole women. He watched in horror as they kneeled, chanted, and expelled their internal organs from their mouths, then took the form of owls and soared off into the night.

Sprague hurried to Fort Brooke with the knowledge of what he had seen, relaying the tale, but by the time reinforcements arrived, all the other soldiers lay dead along the ground or in tents, their hearts removed.

No one ever saw the group of elderly Seminole after that, but they are always remembered in this story of the Dade Massacre.

Before it uses its eerie supernatural abilities to manifest an owl exterior, the Stikini is otherwise indistinguishable from an ordinary human descended from Seminole Indigenous ancestry.

The Stikinct has potential for two distinct personas: that of the human form and that of its monstrous incarnation. Naturally, the human body is that which it projects in society; this may be the more reserved and secretive manifestation of the Stikini's personality.

Stikini's nature as a mage may reject cultural norms for propriety and show little to no regard for social taboos (or those who regard such taboos). The monstrous persona is often the truth behind a human mask of kindness, gentleness, and good intention.

Either way, the first persona is laid to rest when the human form sleeps. That is when the monstrous incarnation of the Stikini comes forth. During this time, the Stikini uses its powers to transform and attack its enemies. Its favored attack is the theft of the enemy's still-beating heart.

When it has obtained the prize it is after, and the Stikini regains its composure to transform back to human, it then eats the bloody heart, after having prepared it in a special magic pot.

Witch Shifting into Crow Gloucester and Louisburg, Massachusetts

Skinwalkers are not the only witches able to shapeshift in American stories. Historically, Caucasian witches could, too. One of these witches was a young woman named Rhines, who was said to cast spells over young men. Another was older woman, Peg Wesson, in 1745, in what is now deserted Dogtown in

Massachusetts. Peg supposedly shifted into the form of a black crow.

Like the crow, she flew, following a detachment of soldiers to Louisburg until one of the soldiers shot the bird down with a silver bullet, made from a button from the soldier's coat. Precisely at that moment, Old Peg back in Gloucester fell and broke her leg, dying afterward. Many claimed they found a silver bullet inside her.

Not saying there are evil witches after you, but you should make sure that both your front and back doors, plus all your windows, are locked tight before you head to bed tonight. That animal or bird in your front yard staring at you just might be a witch out to get you!

Cannibal Shapeshifting Monsters

The Wendigo!
The Wendigo!
I saw it just a friend ago!
Last night, it lurked in Canada;
Tonight, on your veranda!
As you are lolling hammockwise
It contemplates you stomachwise.
~Ogden Nash

Wendigo

Shifting from one shape to another can be done in many ways. By physical means, magical means, and even by possession by a dark spirit to change the body it uses. The wendigo can change the possessed body to become a monster, needing to feed on human flesh as the spirit does. First, it is the giant ogre of legend; second, the human possessed by the wendigo spirit to transform into one themselves; and for a third reason of the cannibal urge itself, acting out a crime or fantasy.

Depending on the many Indigenous Peoples that speak an Algonquian language, including the Abenaki, Siksika, Mi'kmaq, Algonquin,

Ojibwe, and Innu, the spelling and pronunciation of the word "wendigo" or "windigo" differs. The source of the English word is the Ojibwe word wiindigoo. In the Cree language, it is wīhtikōw, also transliterated wetiko. Weendigo, Windego, Wiindgoo, Windgo, Weendigo, Windago, Windiga, Wendego, Windagoo, Widjigo, Wiijigoo, Wijigo, Weejigo, Wìdjigò, Wintigo, Wentigo, Wehndigo, Wentiko, Windgoe, Windgo, and Wintsigo are all alternative versions of the same term.

Other names, such as atchen, chenoo, and kewok, are also commonly used to refer to the wendigo. The Proto-Algonquian term has been reconstructed as wi·nteko·wa, which may have meant "owl." It also means the one who lives alone, a hermit. In the United States, claims of the wendigo being seen or talked about are in Maine, Minnesota, and other states near Minnesota, plus also up in Canada.

Many tales of the wendigo have existed in Algonquian oral history for centuries, long before Europeans arrived in what is now called North America. It's generally associated with the deepest winter—the time of famine.

According to Algonquin legends, the wendigo haunts the northern forests of what are now the United States and Canada, always looking for people to eat.

One tale tells that the wendigo was once a lost hunter. During a brutally cold winter, this man's intense hunger drove him to cannibalism. After feasting on another human's flesh, he transformed into a crazed man-beast, roaming the forest in search of more people to eat.

The story of the wendigo comes from Algonquian folklore, and the exact details vary depending on who you ask. Some people who have claimed to encounter the beast say it's a relative of Bigfoot. But other reports compare the wendigo to a werewolf instead, which is why it is in this book, a spirit taking over a human and changing them into what it is, a cannibalistic monster.

At the turn of the 20th century, the Algonquian tribes blamed many unsolved disappearances of people on wendigo attacks. Some still believe it still is the cause of people disappearing or found chewed on today. I even watched a whole hour about the wendigo on Monsters Attack on the Travel Channel Sunday, December 13, 2020. Interestingly, this frightening creature doesn't have a human heart but one of ice, and that the hearts of those it changes become a block of ice, too.

Another story told of another man, who through hunger or personal failure, broke the taboo against eating human flesh. An evil spirit possessed him and forced him to become insatiably hungry for more—always eating and always starving, transforming into the wendigo.

Just as there are different versions of what it is called, there are many variations on the creature's appearance and powers. A native author and ethnographer named Basil H. Johnston once described the wendigo in his masterwork *The Manitous: The Spiritual World of the Ojibway*, saying, "The Wendigo was gaunt to the point of emaciation, its desiccated skin pulled tightly over its bones. With its bones pushing out over its skin, its complexion the ash gray of death, and its eyes pushed back deep into the sockets; the Wendigo looked like a gaunt skeleton recently disinterred from the grave. What lips it had was tattered and bloody. Unclean and suffering from suppurations of the flesh, the Wendigo gave off a strange and eerie odor of decay and decomposition."

Others describe it with other differences. Sometimes, it's described as exceptionally thin, with the skull and skeleton pushing through its ash-colored, mummy-like skin. Other stories describe the wendigo as a well-fleshed giant who gets proportionately larger the more it eats.

Most wendigos are males. Descriptions of what it looks like or when someone becomes one has it with a gigantic head with a lipless cavern of a mouth (some natives say the creature is lipless as it is so hungry it has eaten its own lips) filled with jagged teeth and has an awful breath and body odor. It makes a sinister hiss from that mouth that one can hear from far away. Its eyes are large and protuberant like an owl's, even dark. Its hands are massive and edged with claws, as long as 12 inches or more. The monster is human-shaped, but it has long legs with its feet ending in one toe that ends with a long, sharp dagger of a nail. This enables the wendigo to slash its victims. According to other legends, it has pointed or animal-like ears with antlers or horns sprouting on its head.

When it howls or roars, the sound is earsplitting! It can also whistle or growl. It seems to be able to make the earth shake, the wind howl, and cause animals to flee. Indigenous tales have said it can devour grizzly bears, all men, and horses in one gulp. The wendigo can tear up trees and leave a path of destruction, even using a tree as a club or walking stick. That it is extraordinarily strong and yet looks cadaverous in many pictures done of it. The wendigo can also swim, so diving into the waters of a lake or river to escape it will not help its victim.

Though it is hard to kill or destroy, one way is by melting its icy heart or, if you can manage to do it, cut off its head. According to some legends, wendigos can be killed with a conventional weapon, such as a club or firearm. Other legends claim that it must be somehow subdued, its icy heart cut out and then melted in a roaring fire. There are also stories that say only a knowledgeable First Nations spiritual leader, a shaman, can dispatch a wendigo with a specific spell and ceremony.

Sometimes, though, the wendigo is depicted as a skeleton-like being made of ice, with its internal organs made of frost. And if two wendigos of the opposite sex meet, they would battle until one is defeated and thrown into a fire to burn down to ashes, except for the heart of ice, which is taken out and beaten down to be thrown back into the fire to be melted. So, there is obviously no mating, for the wendigo is a lonely monster and not sociable. The Cree and Ojibwa call it "the outsider," "He-Who-Walks-Along," or Upayokawitigo, which means "Hermit."

It is considered eternal and that it came before even the Indigenous tribes lived on the land. That besides its cannibal nature, it also causes misfortunes and disasters. It's blamed for tornadoes, windstorms, frosts, terrible snowstorms, famine, mass illnesses, a person going senile or demented, or disappearances of people or anyone freezing to death. It was the catchall monster to blame for a lot of tragedies.

This monster is usually, but not always, endowed with powers, like superhuman strength and stamina that helps it to stalk, overpower, and devour its victims. Wendigos are usually credited with exceptional eyesight, hearing, and sense of smell. They move with the speed of the wind and have the ability to walk across deep snow or even over open water without sinking.

One of its creepiest traits is the ability to mimic human voices. It uses this skill to lure people in and draw them away from civilization. Once they're isolated in the desolate depths of the wilderness, it attacks them and then feasts on them.

This creature is said to have other skills and powers besides stealth. It also knows and uses every inch of its territory and can control the weather through the use of dark magic.

The Ojibwa describes it: "It was a large creature, as tall as a tree, with a lipless mouth and jagged teeth. Its breath was a strange hiss, its footprints full of blood, and it ate any man, woman, or child who ventured into its territory. And those were the lucky ones. Sometimes, the Wendigo chooses to possess a person instead, and then the luckless individual became a Wendigo himself, hunting down those he had once loved and feasting upon their flesh."

It is said even one who does right and everything they can so as not to be possessed by a wendigo, if they are visited in a dream or vision by a wendigo spirit, they can involuntarily transform into one upon awakening. This can happen during a vision quest, for if a wendigo spirit accosts the person and he doesn't expel it forcefully enough, he is doomed to become one at the end of the vision.

Another way to be possessed by a wendigo and become one can be done by sorcery from a member of an enemy tribe. That means he was cursed.

What I also found interesting is that it seems that the Algonquin tribes who believe in the wendigo, like the Southwestern tribes who believe in the skinwalkers, those in the Pacific Northwest who fear the Wechuge, and certain tribes in Alaska who believe in the Kushtaka, are afraid to speak of the monster, for then it would hear them talking about it and might come to them.

In most legends, humans transform into wendigos because of their greed or weakness. Various Indigenous traditions consider wendigos dangerous because of their thirst for blood and their ability to infect otherwise healthy people or communities with evil. Wendigo legends are essentially cautionary tales about isolation and selfishness and the importance of community. Another rough translation of wendigo than the ones I gave earlier in this chapter is "the evil spirit that devours mankind." When it has infiltrated a person's mind, it can turn them into wendigos as well, instilling upon them a similar lust for human flesh.

The first European-written account of the wendigo was by Paul Le Jeune, a Jesuit missionary who lived among the Algonquin people in the early-17th century in what is now Quebec, Canada.

Stories of the wendigo could also be found on the Western frontier in the 1800s, among Plains Indigenous peoples and employees of the Hudson's Bay Company. Some Hudson Bay

Company traders' records describe encounters with Indigenous spiritual leaders descending into "fits" of religious passion. Indigenous peoples often accused these people of being wendigos; the traders sometimes believed them to be mad.

In some cases, community members or relatives of the accused killed the suspected wendigo as a precaution. In one example, three men killed Cree spiritual leader Abishabis after he became greedy and killed an Indigenous family. This made the three men believe that he was a wendigo.

One of the most infamous cases is the story of Swift Runner, an Indigenous man who murdered and ate his whole family during the winter of 1879. The man claimed to be possessed by a "wendigo spirit" at the time of the murders. It didn't matter, for he was still hanged for his crime.

There was a case involving Jack Fiddler, an Oji-Cree chief and medicine man known for his powers at defeating wendigos. Fiddler claimed to have defeated 14 of the monsters during his lifetime. Some of these creatures were said to have been sent by enemy shamans, and others were members of his own band who had been taken with the insatiable, incurable desire to eat human flesh. In the latter case, Fiddler was usually asked by family members to kill an extremely sick loved one before they were possessed by a wendigo.

Fiddler's own brother, Peter Flett, was killed after becoming one when the food ran out on a trading expedition. Hudson's Bay Company traders, the Cree, and missionaries were well aware of the wendigo legend, though they often explained it as a mental illness or superstition. Regardless, several incidents of people turning wendigo and eating human flesh are documented in the records of the company. In 1907, Fiddler and his brother Joseph were arrested by the Canadian authorities for murder. Jack committed suicide, but Joseph was tried and sentenced to life in prison. He ultimately was granted a pardon but died three days later in jail before receiving the news of this pardon.

The vast majority of supposed wendigo sightings happened between the 1800s and 1920s. A wendigo allegedly made a number of appearances near a town called Rosesu in Northern Minnesota during this time. Each time it was reported, an unexpected death followed, and finally, it was seen no more.

There's a place mentioned on Roadtrippers.com, the Cave of the Windigo (how wendigo is spelled in this case, with i instead of e.). It is a cave tucked out of the way on lake Mameigwess in Ontario in Canada. The cave supposedly is the location for a series of strange cave paintings of large men covered in hair, which many believe resemble the mythological creature. Many have traveled to the lake in search of the creature and to take photos of the wall paintings. Wendigo sightings are still reported, near the Cave of the Windigo and around the town of Kenora, where it has allegedly been spotted by traders, trackers, and trappers for decades. Kenora, Ontario, Canada, has been given the title of Wendigo Capital of the World by many. Most recently, in 2019, mysterious howls in the Canadian wilderness led some to question whether they were caused by the infamous man-beast. There are many who still believe that the wendigo roams the woods and the prairies of northern Minnesota and Canada.

Legends of the wendigo reveal much about the beliefs, ways of life, social structures, and traditions of the people who tell these stories. For some, these stories serve as reminders of the importance of community, and even more importantly, about what can happen when individuals are left outside of the community. One recipe for creating a wendigo—extreme hunger, cold, and isolation—were ever-present and threatening facts of life for many First Nations people living in the northern boreal forests. In fact, most wendigo stories began with an individual or small group trapped in the wilderness during the winter without food, for an extended period, alone and in the cold. Wendigos were said to kill lonely travelers or a member of a group and then take on their personality temporarily before eventually killing other humans it encountered.

The creature's legendary greed represented attitudes about sharing in many Indigenous cultures. In the wilderness, human survival often depended on communal cooperation and the sharing of food and possessions. Any individual who refused to share local resources, especially in times of great deprivation, was considered a "monster."

Much like other legendary beasts, the wendigo remains a fixture in pop culture in modern times. Graphic novels (Mathieu Missoffe's *Curse of the Wendigo*, for example), books, short stories, movies, television shows, and comics like Marvel's *Wendigo*. This last one is created by writer Steve Englehart and artist Herb Trimpe, and the monster is the result of a curse that afflicts those who commit acts of cannibalism. It first appeared in the comic, *The Incredible Hulk* #162, released April 1973, and again in the October 1974 issue.

The creature inspired artworks by Norval Morrisseau and literary works by Basil H. Johnston, Margaret Atwood, Tomson Highway, and Joseph Boyden. A wendigo in non-Indigenous literature is Algernon Blackwood's 1910 short story "The Wendigo." Blackwood's work may have influenced subsequent portrayals in mainstream horror fiction, such as August Derleth's "The Thing that Walked on the Wind" and "Ithaqua" (1933 and 1941). In "Mortality and Mercy in Vienna," the short story by Thomas Pynchon, has the plot concerning a character developing Wendigo Syndrome and going on a killing spree. Stephen King's novel *Pet Sematary* mentions the wendigo in connection to the pet cemetery where people buried in it or close to it, to bring back the dead, who attack, kill, even eat the living. Chippewa author Louise Erdrich's novel *The Round House*, winner of the National Book Award, depicts a situation where an individual person becomes a wendigo. You can find this novel, and works of the other authors, by googling or searching out the title at Amazon, BarnesandNoble.com, or through your local library or bookstore.

The wendigo, or its legend, has appeared in various films and television shows, including Dark Was the Night (2014) and Ravenous (1999). It was in other movies like *Wendigo* in 1978, *The Manitou* in 1978, *Ghost Keeper* (1982), *Wendigo* (1995), *Wendigo* (2001), *The Last Winter* (2006), *Wendigo: Bound by Blood* (2010), *Windigo* (2011)—this uses the "i" instead of "e" name version, and *Don't Look* (2018). A wendigo also appears in the 2020 horror film *The Retreat* and in the 2020 horror movie, *Antlers*. Then, there is the short horror film, *The Wendigo*, that you can watch on YouTube at https://www.youtube.com/watch?v=GjbR0BNlWJo.

TV series with wendigos in their episodes include *Teen Wolf, Supernatural, Blood Ties, Charmed, Grimm,* and *Hannibal,* and "Skin and Bones" 2008 episode of *Fear Itself* (2008-2009). A wendigo appeared in Disney's animated *Duck Tales* Christmas special, "Last Christmas!" in which the creatures are described as "poor souls turned into monsters by obsession and desperation." And a wendigo is the main antagonist in the 2015 horror survival video game *Until Dawn*. There are a couple of lakes today named after the beast, including a Lake Windigo on Star Island in Beltrami County in Minnesota and a Windigo Lake in Sawyer County in Wisconsin.

In the early 20th century, the term "wendigo" found its way into the Western medical vocabulary. It was used by early psychiatrists to refer to a mental condition in which patients felt possessed by cannibalistic desires. Oblate Missionary J. E. Saindon was the first to use the term in the 1920s while working in a Cree community in the western James Bay area. He said that he met a woman who claimed that she saw strangers who wanted to kill and devour her. Saindon referred to the woman's mental condition as a "psychoneurosis"—a mental or behavioral disorder characterized by depression and anxiety. Over time, the condition came to be known as the Wendigo Psychosis. It was even written about in a monograph by Morton Teicher, titled Windigo Psychosis, published in 1960.

Maybe one can count serial killers like Jeffrey Dahmer and earlier murderers who

committed cannibalism with this Wendigo
Psychosis.

Enjoy some Indigenous wendigo stories I
have found.

The Baby and the Wendigo

A cold north wind began to blow. The great
Ogemaa heard the wind and understood its
message. The wendigo, a cannibal giant, was
coming to eat all the Anishinaabek in the
village.

Everyone was terrified. However, there was
a little child who offered to save the people.
They all wondered what this little child could
do, as he was only a baby. Nonetheless, he
insisted he would help the Anishinabek.

The baby said he would need an ax and a
piece of liver. Then he would go and meet the
giant. Once he received these, the young child
started on his way.

When he met the giant, he became as tall as
a pine tree. He fought the wendigo and killed
him. When he came home, he told his mother
he had killed the wendigo. She didn't believe
him, so he told her to go and look where he had
killed the monster.

She went and found a toenail as big as a turtle. Then everyone believed that the small child had killed the giant and saved the village.

Later the boy himself turned into a wendigo.

Another Wendigo Tale

One winter, a newly married couple went hunting with other people. When they moved to the hunting grounds, a child was born to them. One day, as they were gazing at him in his cradleboard and talking to him, the child spoke to them. This shocked them, as babies did not talk.

"Where is that manidogisik (Sky Spirit)?" asked the baby. "They say he is very powerful, and someday I am going to visit him."

His mother grabbed him and said, "You should not talk about that manido that way."

A few nights later, the couple went to sleep. The baby slept in his cradleboard between them. But in the middle of the night, the mother awoke to feel uneasy and discovered her baby missing. She woke up her husband, and he got up, started a fire, and looked all over the wigwam for the baby. They searched the neighbor's wigwam next to theirs, but they could not find their child there, either. They lit birchbark torches and searched the community looking for tracks of whoever, whatever, had taken their baby.

They found tiny footprints leading down to the lake. It was halfway down to the lake that they found the cradleboard, and they knew it was their baby himself. He had crawled out of his cradleboard and was headed for the manido. The tracks that led down to the lake became larger than a grownup human's feet, and the parents realized that their child had turned into a wendigo, the terrible ice monster who could eat people.

They found his tracks where he had walked across the lake. The manidogisik had fifty smaller manidog or little people to protect him. When one of these manidogs threw a rock, it was a bolt of lightning. As the wendigo approached, the manidog heard him coming and ran out to meet him, and both began to fight. Finally, they knocked him down with a bolt of lightning. The wendigo fell dead with a noise like a big tree falling. As he lay there, he looked like a big human, but when the people started to chop him up, they found him to be a huge block of ice. They melted down the pieces and found, in the middle of the body, a tiny infant about 6 inches long with a hole in his head where the manidog had hit him. This was the baby who had turned into the wendigo. If the manidog had not killed the wendigo, the monster would have eaten up the whole village.

The Girl and the Wendigo

A wendigo was coming when the villagers saw the kettle swinging wildly back and forth over the fire. No one felt brave or strong enough to challenge the monster, so they sent for a wise old grandmother who lived at the edge of the village.

But when the old woman's little granddaughter heard Grandmother had no power to do anything, she asked the villagers what was wrong. The people moaned that a wendigo was approaching and that everyone would die, so the little girl asked for two sticks of peeled sumac as long as her arms. She took these home with her.

That night, as it turned bitterly cold, the girl told her grandmother to melt a kettle of tallow over the fire. As everyone watched, trees cracked open, and the river froze over. Suddenly, the wendigo, who stood as tall as a white pine tree, came over the hill, a monstrous dog by its side. With a sumac stick gripped in each hand, the little girl ran out to meet him, with two dogs that ran ahead of her and killed the wendigo's dog.

The little girl grew larger until she stood as tall as the wendigo himself. The sumac sticks turned to copper. With one stick, she swung and hit him, knocking him down, and with the other, she crushed his skull. After she killed the monster, the little girl swallowed the hot tallow and shrank down until she was a normal little girl again.

Everyone rushed over to the wendigo's corpse and began to chop him up. He was made of ice, but in the center, they found the body of a man with his skull crushed in. Thankful for what the little girl did, the villagers gave the little girl everything she wanted.

Interesting, in this last tale of the wendigo by the Woodland Indigenous tribes, it is not the fact that the little girl uses magic to grow and shrink again (after all the villagers went to Grandmother for help, so we assume she was teaching the granddaughter), but that she used two sumac sticks that become copper to defeat the wendigo. Like some of the werewolf stories where silver can harm or kill the beast, sumac or copper appears to do this, too. And when it becomes ice at death, and the villagers take the ice apart, we find a human being inside, a hole in his head caused by the copper-sumac stick. Just like a silver bullet or sword when struck in the werewolf's heart or severing the neck, has the monster become once more the human person.

The next time you decide to visit the northwest, to one of the states there, you might take precautions when hiking in the woods. A very hungry wendigo may be stalking among the trees, and you just might be its next meal.

Wendigos are not the only man-eating spirits and creatures in Indigenous legends, as you will learn as you continue to read.

The Wechuge
Pacific Northwest (Oregon and Washington)

The wechuge is a man-eating creature or evil spirit like a woodland ogre, appearing in the Athabaskan people's legends and some other peoples of the Pacific Northwest. Wechuge is pronounced "way-chu-gay."

In Beaver (from the Dane-zaa) mythology, a person has been possessed or overwhelmed by the power of one of the ancient giant spirit animals—related to becoming "too strong".

These enormous animals were crafty, intelligent, powerful, and somehow retained their power despite being transformed into the present day's normal-sized animals.

Another tribe of the Peace River region in western Canada (also the Dane-zaa), believed that one could become wechuge by breaking a taboo and becoming "too strong". Examples of these taboos include a person having a photo taken with a flash, listening to music made with a stretched string or hide (such as guitar music), or eating meat with fly eggs in it. Like the wendigo, the wechuge seeks to eat people, attempting to lure them away from their fellows by cunning. It is made of ice and extraordinarily strong in one folktale and is only killed by being thrown on a campfire and kept there overnight until it has melted. Being a wechuge is considered a curse and a punishment, as they are destructive and cannibalistic creatures.

Descriptions of the wechuge vary; these creatures' stories have them as malevolent, cannibalistic, supernatural beings.

There is a story by Dennis Culver, titled "Prey for Wechuge," you can listen to on YouTube at *Something Scary* (which is a podcast, too) at
https://www.youtube.com/watch?v=kijZSkyqWpU.

Mhuwe
Delaware

Like the wendigo and the wechuge, the Mhuwe is a large, hairy monster that feeds on human flesh. A Delaware Indigenous Peoples legend, Mhuwes were once human beings who became cannibals and shifted into the monster form. I learned of one tale from an Indigenous website, native-languages.org, where one tribe took one of these beings and began feeding it vegetables, fruits, and cooked meats until the creature changed back to human.

Feline Shapeshifters

There is in some cases a psychic need to loose evil upon the world, and all of us carry within us a desire for death. You fear the panther, yet you're drawn to him, again and again. Couldn't you turn to him as an instrument of death?
~Cat People

Ailuranthropy comes from the Greek words ailouros, meaning "cat", and anthropos, meaning "human," and refers to human/feline transformations or other beings that combine feline and human characteristics. Its root word is ailurophobia, the most common term for a phobia of cats, plus ailuranthrope is a lesser-known term that refers to a feline therianthrope.

Depending on the story in question, the species involved can be a domestic cat, a tiger, a lion, a leopard, a lynx, or any other type of cat, including some that are purely mythical felines.

European folklore usually depicts werecats as people who transform into domestic cats. Some European werecats became giant domestic cats or panthers. They are generally labeled witches, even though they may have no magical ability other than self-transformation. During the European witch trials, all shapeshifters, including werewolves, were considered witches whether they were male or female.

African legends describe werelions, werepanthers, or wereleopards. In leopards, this is often because the creature is a leopard deity masquerading as a human. When these gods mate with humans and offspring are produced, these children sometimes grow up to be those who don't transform but may have other powers. In reference to those who turn into lions, the ability is often associated with royalty. Such a being may have been a king or queen in a former life.

In Africa, there are folk tales that speak of the "Nunda," or the "Mngwa," a big cat of immense size that stalks villages at night. Many of these tales say it is more ferocious than a lion and more agile than a leopard. There is the belief in the Nunda to be a variation of therianthrope that, by day, is a human, but by night becomes the werecat. There is no actual evidence and documentation that such a creature ever existed. Still, in 1938, a British Explorer named William Hichens, working in Tanzania, was told by locals that a monstrous cat had been attacking people at night. They claimed they found colossal paw prints, which were much larger than any known big cat, but Hichens dismissed the case, believing it more likely to be a lion with gigantism.

Mainland Asian werecats usually become tigers. In India, the weretiger is often a dangerous sorcerer, portrayed as a menace to livestock, who might at any time turn to man-eating. These tales traveled through the rest of India and into Persia through travelers who encountered India's royal Bengal tigers and then further west.

Chinese legends often describe weretigers as the victims of either a hereditary curse or a vindictive ghost. Ancient teachings held that every race except the Han Chinese were animals in disguise. There was nothing extraordinary about some of these false humans reverting to their true natures. Alternatively, the ghosts of people who had been killed by tigers could become an evil supernatural being known as "Chang" (伥), devoting all their energy to making sure that tigers killed more humans. Some of these ghosts were responsible for transforming ordinary humans into man-eating weretigers.

In Japanese folklore, there are creatures called bakeneko, similar to kitsune (fox spirits) and bake-danuki (Japanese raccoon-dog spirits). In Thailand, a tiger that eats many humans may become a weretiger. There are also other types of weretigers, such as sorcerers with incredible powers who can change their form to become animals.

In both Indonesia and Malaysia, there is another kind of weretiger, known as Harimau jadian. In Malaysia, descriptions of Bajangs have them as vampiric or demonic werecats. In the central area of the Indonesian island of Java, the power of transformation is regarded as due to inheritance, the use of spells, fasting and willpower, charms, etc. Save when it is hungry or has just cause for revenge, this creature is not hostile to man; in fact, it takes its animal form only at night and guards the plantations against wild pigs. Variants of this belief assert that the shapeshifter does not recognize his friends unless they call him by name or that he goes out as a mendicant and transforms himself to take vengeance on those who refuse him alms. Somewhat similar is the Khonds' belief, who believe that the tiger is friendly, and he reserves his wrath only for their enemies. A man is said to take the form of a tiger to wreak a just vengeance.

The foremost were-animal in pre-Columbian Mesoamerican cultures is the were-jaguar. It is associated with the veneration of the jaguar. Priests and shamans among the various peoples follow this tradition by wearing jaguars' skins to "become" a were-jaguar. Among the Aztecs, an entire class of specialized warriors dressed in the jaguar skins were called "jaguar warriors" or "jaguar knights." Depictions of the jaguar and the were-jaguar are among the most common motifs among the artifacts of the ancient Mesoamerican civilizations.

In the 11th edition of the *Encyclopaedia Britannica* (1911), Thomas wrote that according to Carl Friedrich Philipp von Martius (1794–1868), the Canaima was a human being who employed poison to carry out his function as blood avenger. Those other authorities represent the Canaima as a jaguar, either an avenger of blood or the familiar of a cannibalistic sorcerer. He also mentioned that in 1911, some Europeans in Brazil believed that the seventh child of the same sex in unbroken succession becomes a were-man or woman and takes the form of a horse, goat, jaguar, or pig.

Urban legends in the United States tell of encounters with feline bipeds, similar to the Bigfoot, having cat heads, tails, and paws. Feline bipeds are classified as a part of cryptozoology but are also interpreted as werecats. Then there are the legends of Indigenous Peoples from the Southeastern region about the Wampus Cat.

Assertions of werecats truly existing and having an origin in supernatural or religious realities have been common for centuries, with these beliefs often hard to separate from folklore. In the 19th century, occultist J. C. Street asserted that cat and dog transformations for real happened by manipulating the "ethereal fluid" that human bodies are supposedly floating in. The Catholic witch-hunting manual, the *Malleus Maleficarum*, asserted that witches could turn into cats but that their transformations were illusions created by demons. New Age author John Perkins stated that every person could shapeshift into "jaguars, bushes, or any other form" by using mental power. Occultist Rosalyn Greene claims that werecats called "cat shifters" exist as part of a "shifter subculture" or underground New Age religion based on lycanthropy and related beliefs.

The 1942 Val Lewton film *Cat People* and its 1982 remake both feature female shape-changers: first Simone Simon and then Nastassja Kinski in a highly sexualized role. The 1982 version also includes Malcolm McDowell as her brother, also a shape-changer.

The titular creatures in the horror film *Sleepwalkers* (written by Stephen King) are werecats who have psychic abilities and can hide disguised within human society. They are also energy vampires who must feed on the life-force of virgin women to survive. Their weakness is domestic cats, which can see through their illusions and destroy them via scratching.

Panther Being
Illinois

Dogman appears not to be the only such cryptid encountered in this part of the country. There is a panther-like being, too. At least in the Devil's Kitchen of the Shawnee National Forest in Southern Illinois.

Before we go into the stories of the cryptids that stalk Illinois, let's learn something about the state. The word Illinois comes from the French word meaning Illini or Land of Illini.

Illini is an Algonquin word meaning men or warriors. Illinois was discovered by Europeans in 1673, settled in 1720, and became part of the Union on December 3, 1818.

Thousands of years before the first White man stepped on the land, Paleo-Indians, a nomadic people, and their descendants, archaic "Indians", explored and inhabited Illinois. Woodland Peoples were their descendants. By 900 AD, Middle Mississippi Peoples succeeded the Woodland Peoples, and they built large earthen mounds and developed complex urban areas. These cities disappeared, possibly because of overpopulation, disease, and exhaustion of resources. The descendants of the Mississippians were the Illiniwek tribes of the 17th, 18th, and 19th centuries. After years of losing land and wars with other Indigenous groups and European colonists, they moved the Illiniweks to a Kansas reservation.

Illinois is surrounded by bodies of water on nearly every border: the Mississippi River to the west, the Ohio and Wabash Rivers to the south, and Lake Michigan to the North. The highest point in Illinois is Charles Mound in JoDaviess County, its elevation being 1,235 feet. The lowest point is in Cairo, Alexander County.

By the 2000 census, Illinois had the sixth largest population of the fifty states. Chicago, in terms of population, is the third-largest city in the country.

So, where do panthers that can walk bipedally figure in all of this? It appears werepanthers, just like dogman, might also exist among us.

The first story happened in 1917, where a "puma" jumped and scratched a Monticello butler. Then near Decatur, on the night of July 29 that same year, a similar creature attacked an automobile. A black panther was seen near Coulter's Mill in northern Macon County. At the time, the game warden, Paul G. Myers, shot at it and hit it in the flank, but its body was never recovered.

There were tales told about a mountain lion spooking cattle and that it killed a calf in southeastern Lawrence County in May 1963. Later that summer, a state trooper fired at a black panther in Saline County. Reports of a large black cat-like animal coming out of the woods near Decatur to gobble up the sack lunch dropped by one of a group of fleeing children happened in June 1963.

This created problems for the State of Illinois Department of Conservation. The mountain lion/puma/panther has been officially extinct in Illinois since 1850. And there had never been a black version of the only sizeable American cat in the United States. They would explain it away as a wolf, a black calf, an ordinary black cat, or a dog.

The Shawnee National Forest has numerous stories of cryptids seen and heard there. The Shawnee Forest stretches from the eastern border along the Ohio River to the western and the Mississippi, down to where the great rivers meet, like a sylvan patch of pubic hair on the trunk of the state. The area is known for rolling hills, steep bluffs, high hills, and dark hollows.

The government bought the land in 1939 for a national forest. Most of the trees that blanket the landscape today were planted at that time. When the settlers came, this was old growth forest, teeming with predators like bears, wolves, mountain lions, and rattlesnakes. Today the super predators are gone, except for a few wolves that were reintroduced to the area, and of course, snakes. Plus, maybe this panther cryptid, Bigfoot, and other creatures.

But a panther had been seen in this area as told on the ninth episode of the third season of *Monsters and Mysteries in America*. I didn't think much at the time when I watched this section. It was what it did to one witness in the segment that I knew it had to be added to this book!

As a 19-year-old, Mike Busby worked late at the garage where he was employed in April 1970. Finished finally, he drove his Chevy on Route 3 to Olive Branch to pick up his new bride from her place of work.

It was as he passed through the Shawnee National Forest that his automobile quit running. He got out and had released the hood latch when he heard a noise on his left. He turned and was startled to see two quarter-sized, almond-shaped, greenish glowing eyes staring at him from the woods. Suddenly, something large and black as the night leaped upon him, knocking him on his back. To his horror, Mike saw a massive black panther.

It reared over him, snarling, and began shredding his shirt. It scratched him and even bit him. The more Mike screamed, the more it growled louder. Finally, the lights of an oncoming truck stopped the beast.

Suddenly, it stood up on its hind legs and bolted into the trees, all of this lit up by the other car's lights. The truck's driver ran over to Mike, saying' "My God! What was that?" The man had seen the panther running away bipedally.

Mike suffered scratches and a bite on his arms, back, chest, neck, and face. The truck driver helped Mike to his car, where Mike drove to St. Mary's Hospital in Cairo, followed by the other man.

The police did talk to him. They didn't believe it was a panther at all, but some wolf, no matter what Mike kept telling them. A few weeks later, an Alexander County sheriff killed a wolf along Route 3, and the report on Mike was considered closed. But Mike knew that a black panther had attacked him, enough to years later talk about it on the paranormal reality TV show in 2015.

On July 9th, three young adults, Don Ennis, Beecher Lamb, Larry Faircloth, and Bob Hardwick—all 18—went camping a mile south of Farmer City near Salt Creek. Their campsite, often used as a lovers' lane, was very isolated. Before the night was over, they would realize just how remote it was.

At about 10:30 P.M., they heard something moving in the tall grass as they sat around the campfire. When "it" moved between them and their tent, Lamb decided to turn his car lights on. The thing, whose widely separated eyes gleamed at them, was squatting by the tent before it ran off on two legs—the young men left in a big hurry themselves. Ennis, who had one foot in a cast because of a broken ankle, left his crutches behind.

Soon word about the Farmer City "monster" spread. On Friday, July 10, more than 10 people claimed to have seen a pair of glowing eyes near the site of the first sighting. At least 15 people swore they had seen a furry creature in the same area. Witnesses told how "it" seemed to be attracted by the sound of loud radio music and campfires.

Police Officer Robert Hayslip of Farmer City decided to check out the stories of the monster. He went out to the campsite/lovers' lane area early Wednesday morning, July 15, between two and three o'clock. Hayslip heard something running through the grass. He said, "Out of the corner of my eye, I could see these two extremely bright eyes, just like it was standing there watching me." As he turned toward it, he said, it disappeared.

About six in the morning, Hayslip again visited the site. He found that the heavy steel grommets in a tent that had been intact earlier were now ripped out, plus nearby, he found a quilt torn to shreds.

In the end, Hayslip decided that the so-called monster was nothing more than a Shetland pony, and he didn't investigate further.

Besides the Mike Busby story, the episode had another, more modern story about two young men driving through the forest when one of them saw a black mass ahead on the road. As they approached closer, both men saw a black panther in the headlights, crossing the road to the other side, where it vanished into the woods.

Next time you are driving in Illinois, primarily through the Shawnee National Forest, don't be in shock if you catch a glimpse of a black panther strolling upright across the road. It won't give you bad luck, not unless you pull over and get out to check.

Catman Haunting Former Bong Air Base Kansasville, Wisconsin

Do you think UFOs might be the only things of paranormal nature encountered on airbases? It appears even dogmen might be there, too, mostly in places like Bong Air Base from World

War II, which has been abandoned for a long time and became a 4000-acre wildlife preserve named Richard Bong State Recreation Area. The giant underground tunnels from when it was a base are still there, sealed off to humans but rumored to have paranormal activities, and where strange creatures are encountered, such as canines and even big cats that shouldn't be there.

Stephen D. Sullivan, an author, and his wife, each encountered something large and black in their vehicles' headlights on different visits. Sullivan had his encounter on July 14, 2014, as he was driving his son and daughter home in the evening. It ran on all fours and seemed as large as a German Shepherd, except it had a long tail. He couldn't be sure if it was a wolf, dog, coyote, or even a large cat.

The second sighting happened to his wife returning home with the kids five nights later. With only a glimpse of a black rump and long tail, she couldn't be sure if it was a large cat, like a panther (since mountain lions are not black) or some canine.

Even stranger, both saw a man in black jogger clothing and a black knit hat jogging in the same area after their encounters. It recalled "Men in Black;" connected to UFO sightings or even mystery animals. The man vanished after several weeks.

Strangely enough, the park has had UFO sightings, strange lights, and cultist activity along Highway 75. It even has ancient Adena-era mounds. The Adena people were a group of well-organized Indigenous Peoples who lived in parts of what is present-day Ohio, Indiana, Wisconsin, West Virginia, Kentucky, Pennsylvania, Maryland, and New York around 1000 B.C. to about 1 A.D. The only lasting traces of Adena culture still seen are in the remains of their substantial earthworks, which only a small number of the remains survive to today. These mounds generally ranged from 20 feet to 300 feet in diameter and served as burial structures, ceremonial sites, historical markers, and possibly gathering places.

Most sightings of upright beasts or even on all fours in Wisconsin have been canines, but again, as in the *Mysteries and Monsters* episode, canine creatures are not the only types seen.

Now some might say that maybe it was a cougar (also called a puma, panther, or mountain lion), but zoologists insist that black or melanistic mountain lions do not exist. Still, people see out-of-place black panther-sized beasts the world over. So, what did these witnesses see?

The Wampus Cat
Virginia, West Virginia, North Carolina, Kentucky, and Tennessee

One may hear the chilling shrieks of the Wampus Cat throughout the Appalachian region of the American Southeast in the night. Bloodthirsty monstrosities, they seem filled with palpable anger and hatred. Wampus Cats are known to mutilate and butcher entire herds of livestock, not to sate any hunger, but for pure pleasure. The random things left out in the yard at night—buckets, rakes, clothes hanging on a line—are knocked over or even destroyed. The folks who live in the rural areas hide in their homes, as they know what it is. They say that it's the Wampus Cat.

Folklore says Wampus Cats were once witches but became cursed with an unholy, bestial form as punishment for pursuing secrets no one should ever know. And it is rumored that the Wampus Cat is always female. But again, maybe it is a form the witch may transform into to steal or kill cattle and other animals owned by people, like witches have done in many Indigenous Tribes' tales.

I know a horror author, Stephen Mark Rainey, who mentioned the Wampus Cat myth on his blog. He always assumed that it only existed in Tennessee until he heard the stories about it in North Carolina. The creature also stalks in Virginia. Its stories are told mainly in the western and southwestern sections of the state. Plus, there is a story connected to West Virginia. Once a part of Virginia before the Civil War, this can be considered a Virginian story, depending on when it was told.

From a distance, witnesses had mistaken the Wampus Cat for an overly large, grotesque monkey. Sometimes, some call it another cryptid, the Devil Monkey. But up close, one can see the horrid truth.

The head is something like that of a feline, with baleful red eyes and slavering jaws. Its body is vaguely anthropoid and covered in layers of thick, glossy fur. Beneath the layers, there is a hint of something mockingly like that of the human female form. The Wampus Cat carries a bushy-tail behind its body, which it swishes angrily.

While the monster can walk upright, it prefers to make astonishing leaps using its hind legs. Both forepaws and hind legs conceal claws that could quickly eviscerate a man. A repugnant odor comes off the monster, a noxious mix of sulfur and an animal in heat. Like the witches of folklore, Wampus Cats hunt in packs of three. A Wampus Cat will never be alone; her companions are always watching nearby.

One story is an old Cherokee legend about how the Wampus Cat came to be. There was once a beautiful Cherokee woman, whose husband would often leave the village with the other men to hunt and bring back food. Before each trip, the men would gather in the woods to ask forgiveness for the lives of the animals they were about to take and to seek supernatural help in their task. But women were forbidden from ever seeing these sacred rites.

Her curiosity consumed her, and she wanted to know the secret magic. She begged and begged her husband to reveal the rites to her, but he always refused. One night, as the men set out into the forest, she wrapped herself in a cougar skin and quietly crept through the woods, tracking them. She came upon the clearing in the forest where the men gathered around a fire. She hid behind a rock and watched, enthralled, finally seeing the secrets she had so long desired to see. She crept closer and closer to the men in the circle, hoping to catch everything when the sorcerer leading the rituals spotted her. He saw through her disguise that she was a woman and not a cougar. The men of the tribe grabbed her and dragged her into the circle.

To punish her for breaking the taboo, the sorcerer cast a spell on the woman. The cougar skin she wrapped herself in merged with hers and became her skin. She shifted into a strange mix of cougar and human and became cursed to live forever alone in the woods, never again enjoying human company.

That is why the Wampus Cat roams the Appalachian Mountains at night, forever wandering and ever alone in the mountains. She steals animals or ruins things on the farms, acting out her anger and resentment from being cut off from the rest of humanity and never able to rejoin.

Another version of the Wampus Cat story has it as a beast terrorizing the Cherokee. One brave tried to kill it, but he saw it and went insane. His wife put on a mask and went to find the monster, and when she found it, she snuck up behind it and screamed. The creature turned around, saw her, and fled, frightened. To this day, some claim to have seen the woman's spirit, still wearing the mask, and she screams as now she is the Wampus Cat.

The Wampus Cat is said to stalk the hills, looking for animals to steal. When the moon is full, you will hear her howl. If you're camping in the woods and hear her piercing wail, beware. She may hunt you.

In another tale, a witch attempted to shapeshift into a cat when local villagers caught her. She fled, doomed to be half cat, half woman forever.

Whatever the truth is, farmers still tell of their cattle disappearing, never to be found, or dying mysteriously, and they still blame it on the Wampus Cat.

A story about this creature happened to Tim Smith in modern-day Bristol, Virginia.

He was in downtown Abingdon one night when he saw two eyes looking at him through some iron steps. He thought they were the eyes of a cat—not the eyes of some house cat, but a much larger animal.

He yelled at it, and it hissed at him before something as large as a mountain lion bolted into the darkness. Not just him, but his wife saw the creature, too. What freaked them out is that it ran away on its hind legs!

Another sighting from the internet that L.B. Taylor found for his book, *Monsters of Virginia*, occurred in the Blue Ridge Mountains. A man was camping with some friends. One of the friends screamed as they were gathering wood for their campfire. The other man stabbed his flashlight at the trees and saw something standing nearby; it didn't look like a Bigfoot or any primate. And it didn't look like a bear, either.

It had hooked a paw onto his buddy, who was struggling to get free. It looked like a 5-foot-tall cat on its hind legs, and when his light hit it, it let go of his friend and took off on those, not on all four as a typical cat would. His friend had five puncture marks on his shoulder and scratches on his head, and he bubbled that the "cat" kept trying to bite at his neck.

Another story connected to West Virginia is about a man named Jinx Johnson. Big and British, nothing scared him, at least, not until he met the Wampus Cat.

The Wampus Cat was an old witch woman who lived in the hills alone. People there suspected her of using magic to steal their farm animals. She did this by going to a neighbor's house in the form of a house cat and let in by the door where she hid until nighttime. When everyone in the home went to bed, she cast a spell to keep them asleep so that she could steal their animals. She also took personal things of the family to keep casting the enchantment, such as locks of their hair, personal objects, or anything to aid her in doing what she needed to keep doing.

Even though never caught, the locals devised a plan to capture her, and they hid in one barn; and when she came inside to get the livestock, they all jumped her, and it shocked her enough to stay as half woman, half cat. She escaped and ended up roaming the woods and nearby mountains at night, prowling for livestock and children.

This is where Jinx comes into this story.

He was out hunting raccoons one night with his dogs when he heard unearthly howls. The sounds frightened his dogs, who ran away and never came back when he called for them. Jinx tripped over a root of a tree, or maybe it was a rock—it was that dark—and his rifle flew out of his hands. As he tried to find the weapon, a terrible stench slammed into his nostrils. He heard growling and looked up to see the Wampus Cat towering over him. Its eyes glowed yellow, and it opened its mouth to howl again, revealing large, sharp fangs. Jinx's heart drummed against his chest and he began shaking.

Not having his gun, Jinx ran for his life. He prayed he would make it home as he could feel the beast's hot breath on the back of his neck. When he arrived home, he ran indoors, never so glad he'd left the place unlocked. The door slammed behind him—he made sure to slide the locks home—and he grabbed his bible to read it. As he read all night, the Wampus Cat kept howling. Finally, at daybreak, it left. Jinx never went coon hunting at night after that. He never found out who the cat was, either, but he was happy to be alive and never see it again.

An interesting, amusing note to Wampus Cat was back in the 1920s when men in the southern states' mountains were making moonshine. They used the legend of the monster for their benefit. Whenever they brewed a batch of the illegal whiskey, they would shoot a rifle into the air to let others know it was ready, and the men would tell their wives they were off to hunt a Wampus Cat sighted in the area.

Other Odd Shapeshifting Beings

*His eyes went to predatory mode, following my
every movement.
The gold flecks in his eyes gleamed.*
~Kenya Wright

Elk Man
Wichita Mountains National Wildlife Refuge, Oklahoma

Oklahoma has more than werewolves and
dogmen residing in the state; it has an elk man,
too. At least it did in 2012, in the Wichita
Mountains National Wildlife Refuge.

Rick, a photographer, caught sight of it
when he and a friend were in the park, shooting
photos of stars in the night sky at 10 at night.
Suddenly, a parade of wildlife began moving
before them: coyotes, bison, and a herd of elk.
Had something spooked them? At that moment,
a bunch of feral hogs ran past, pretty close, but
oblivious to the humans.

Nothing else, but the air appeared to have
grown thick with pressure, ominous, no sound
at all, and the two men hastily packed

everything into the trunk of their vehicle. Just as they were about to leave, the headlights on and the motor running, they saw what had spooked all the wildlife. Light from the car lit up a tall human figure. Except it had an elk's head with a set of antlers on its neck! It looked at them, and both saw it had red eyes. Was that a mask? Rick didn't know; all he felt was an overwhelming need to get out of there, so he punched the accelerator and zoomed down the road. He never went back to see if it was just a man in a mask, and he didn't want to find out otherwise.

Not in Oklahoma, but Indigenous Peoples consider the elk a clan animal. The Lakota consider the elk a member of the four-legged nation and would not be called an "animal." Albert White Hat, a Sičháŋǧu Lakota and Lakota language teacher, said, "We don't have a word for 'animal' in our language. [An] Animal, as I understand, means a second-class citizen that doesn't have a mind."

To some Pacific Northwest tribes, elk are considered to be particular protectors of women, and in some legends, elk lead women who had been captured by enemy warriors back to their homes. Other tribes use the elk's symbolism of bravery and masculinity as the premise behind their warrior societies, which, for tribes like the Blackfeet of Montana, are still active today.

Can they be used as an animal to possess and become an elk person, or even transform to become an Elkman?

Elk man, or at least an elk woman, is figured in a horror novel, *The Only Good Indians*, by Blackfeet horror author, Stephen Graham Jones. It has an elk who lost her calf due to four Indigenous friends and shifts to a human form to get revenge. At times, she has an elk head on a human body, but other times, she becomes her elk self.

Jones reinterpreted a Blackfeet legend about the elk cow, how her whole herd jumped from a steep bluff and were killed, but she refused to do that because she was heavy with her calf. She did live, though, and the old man in the legend lost his dead elks to wolves, and the mice ate the inside of the elk tongues he cut out and hung up, so he starved. But Jones changed the legend and wrote an excellent horror story.

Boar Man
Wichita Mountains National Wildlife Refuge in Oklahoma

It seems that the Elk Man is not the only weird creature in the Wichita Mountains National Wildlife Refuge. There are stories about a boar man, too.

President William McKinley designated the preserve in 1901 to protect the wildlife and flora. The government planted the 16-acre Parallel Forest of 20,000 red cedar trees to combat the Dust Bowl during the Great Depression. It has 22,400 acres of land, enough space for even cryptids and shapeshifters to hide within.

The Parallel Forest has a haunted, eerie feeling about it. More so, that the Boar Man lives there. This creature has been seen by many for a long time. One story says he looks like a strong middle-aged man with piggish eyes. Standing between 6- and 8-foot-tall, he wears a hog's skin and carries a wild boar's tusk that he uses when he attacks his victims. The other reports, though, have him metamorphosing into an actual gigantic wild hog. Whatever guise the creature uses, anyone foolish enough to get close gets gored.

There is a third tale connected to him—that he is an old man who uses a boar tusk to pierce a victim's flesh and then uses black magic to steal their youth. Maybe using black magic enables him to shift into a wild boar, and with his tucks, he can siphon from the young men to remain young.

Wisconsin Goatman

Although Prince George, Maryland, and Prince George, Virginia have tales of the Goatman, they all mention stories of mad science experiments, making a half man and half goat satyr where it stalks its victims wielding an ax. The folklore in Wisconsin Goatman comes from the late 1800s, where it has a goat walking on its two hind legs, and even the later story from 2003 sounded more like an upright goat than the half-man, half-goat satyr.

The 2003 incident concerned two witnesses driving along Hogsback Road when they had to stop as a goat on its two hind legs crossed from one side of the road to the other in front of their vehicle, disappearing among the trees. They saw something the size of a man with large, muscular legs and tiny arms, a goat's head, and form. Was this a shapeshifter?

Shapeshifting Beings of Indigenous Myths and Legends

When one sits in the Hoop of the People,
One must be responsible because
All of Creation is related.
And the hurt of the one is the hurt of all.
And the honor of one is the honor of all. And
whatever we do affects everything in the
universe.
~White Buffalo Calf Woman

Buffalo at Richmond Metro Zoo in Mosley, Virginia

White Buffalo Woman (*Ptesan-Wi*)
Lakota (Sioux)

In a Lakota legend, this creature appears as a woman who shapeshifts into a white bison.

She is known as Buffalo Calf Woman, White Buffalo Cow Woman, or White Buffalo Calf Maiden.

There was a great famine and the Lakota chief sent out two scouts to hunt for food. They left camp with dogs still yawning, setting out across the plain, accompanied by the yellow meadowlark song.

After a while, the day began to grow warm. Crickets chirruped in the waving grass; prairie dogs darted their holes as the hunters approached but they spotted no real game. So, the young men made towards a little hill to see further across the vast expanse of level prairie.

Reaching it, they shielded their eyes and scanned the distance, but beheld coming out of the growing heat haze something bright, walking on two legs, not four. Soon they recognized her as a beautiful woman in shining white buckskin, wonderfully decorated with sacred designs in rainbow-colored porcupine quills. She had a bundle on her back and carried a fan of fragrant sage leaves in her hand. Her jet-black hair hung loose, except for a single strand tied with buffalo fur. Her eyes were full of light and power.

One of the two scouts was filled with burning desire, "What a woman!" he said. "And all alone on the prairie. I'm going to make the most of this!"

"You fool," said the other, "this woman is holy."

He ignored the other's advice and still approached the woman when she beckoned. A cloud enclosed him and her after he grabbed her, and he turned into a pile of bones. The second man came up to the woman, and although he was frightened, the woman explained that she was *wakan*, or holy, and why she had appeared to him.

"I come to your people with a message from *Tatanka Oyate*, (this meant in Lakota the Buffalo Nation). Return to your chief and tell him what you have seen. Tell him to prepare a tipi large enough for all his people and to get ready for my coming."

When the White Buffalo Calf Woman arrived, she brought the White Buffalo Calf *chanupa* (the sacred pipe) and taught them seven sacred ways to pray. Before she left, she told them that she would return to restore harmony and spirituality to a troubled world. She rolled upon the earth four times, changing color each time, and transformed into a white buffalo calf before she vanished. Suddenly, many, many herds of buffalo surrounded the camps. The birth of a white buffalo calf signifies that their prayers are heard, and the prophecy promises are being fulfilled.

The American buffalo, or bison, is a symbol of abundance and manifestation, often linked to creation and medicine, and are bringers of sacred messages from the ancestors. The lesson learned by the Lakota that day is that one does not have to struggle to survive if the right prayer joins the right action. The birth of a sacred white buffalo is a sign of hope and an indication of good times to come.

White buffalo are scarce; the National Bison Association has estimated that they only occur in approximately one out of every 10 million births.

Bison were hunted almost to extinction in the 19th century, and less than a hundred remained in the wild by the late 1880s, as people pursued them for their skins and tongues, leaving the rest of them left to decay. After the animals rotted, their bones were collected and shipped back east in large quantities.

Buffalo generally reach their mature size at 5 to 6 years old and can live for over 30 years. To honor such an iconic and resilient species, Congress passed the National Bison Legacy Act on April 28, 2016, making the bison a U.S. symbol of unity, resilience, and healthy landscapes and communities. The Act recognizes the historical, cultural, and economic importance of bison. Buffalo comes from the French for beef animal or ox, "boeuf" and bison come from the Greek word for beef or ox.

Deer at Richmond Metro Zoo in Mosley, Virginia

Deer Woman

Deer Woman is also known as the Deer Lady, a deer spirit of the Eastern Woodlands and Central Plains tribes. She is associated with fertility and love. Like many Indigenous animal spirits, Deer Woman is sometimes depicted in animal form, other times in human form, and sometimes as a mixture between the two, with just hooves and brown eyes or the lower body of a doe and upper half of a human woman.

Although Deer Woman was usually considered a benign spirit who might help women conceive children, some stories portray her as a more dangerous being. She seduces men, especially adulterous or promiscuous men, and leads them to their deaths by trampling on them with her hooves or leaving them to pine away from lovesickness.

Among contemporary Indigenous Peoples of Oklahoma, Deer Woman often plays a "bogeyman" sort of role, said to trample incautious people to death, especially girl-crazy young men or disobedient children. Some people say that this more violent version of Deer Woman is a human woman who either transformed into a deer after being raped or brought back to life by the original Deer Woman spirit after being murdered. Others say she is the same Deer Woman, only changing her cause to revenge.

In the Lakota (Sioux) versions of Deer Woman, she doesn't kill men; instead, she takes their soul so that he is lost for the rest of his life. As to the women, Deer Woman spirits them away, never seen again. In these stories, the description of Deer Woman is as a black-tailed deer.

Deer Woman stories are found in many Indigenous tribal lore, told to young children or young adults and preteens in tribes like the Sioux, Ojibwe, Ponca, the Omaha people, Cherokee, Muscogee, Seminole, Choctaw, the Otoe tribe, Osage, the Pawnee people, and the Iroquois.

Deer Woman is one of the Little People: among the Cherokee, they are called *Ani Yunwitsandsdi.* In other words, not unlike the fairies of Celtic and European legends.

Cherokee/Muskogee/Seminole/Choctaw tales are told like this: A beautiful young woman meets a young man and entrances him into a sexual relationship. The woman is so beautiful that the young man is often swayed by her beauty away from family, home, and community. If the young man is so entranced as not to notice the young woman's feet—which in the case of Deer Woman are hooves—then he falls under her spell and stays with her forever, wasting away into depression, despair, prostitution, and ultimately, death.

In Ojibwe tradition, she can be banished with chanting and tobacco. Others claim that Deer Women's spell can be broken if one notices her cloven hooves, and then she runs away.

Some other stories and traditions describe Deer Woman's sighting as a personal transformation sign or a warning. Deer Woman is also said to be fond of dancing and sometimes joins a communal dance unnoticed, leaving when the drum beating ceases. Or she'll be at the pow wow all night as a beautiful woman, and the last dance is the rabbit dance, and it's the dance where the lady picks the man. And she'll choose whichever young man she wants, and he'll dance with her, and Deer Woman gets him to take her home. Once they make it to his house, she turns back into a deer. When dancing with a girl that you don't know, or even a girl you do know, the lore says to always check her feet because when a Deer Woman shapeshifts, her feet remain the cloven hooves of a deer.

Her story has many variations, describing her as everything from Nunnehi in Cherokee stories to a witch or normal human. She is associated with fertility and love in her more beneficent aspect but has quite a dark side when crossed.

Deer play a lesser role in the mythology of Indigenous tribes from other parts of the US and Canada, sometimes figuring as a messenger or a fertility spirit. In the Tlingit tribe of the Northwest Coast, deer symbolize peace and are associated with ambassadors. There is even an Algonquian legend about a jealous man who nearly turns his girlfriend into a deer, so a sort of shapeshifter tale.

Deer Woman was a character on *Showtime's Masters of Horror*, the episode directed by John Landis, which originally aired December 9, 2005. You can find the video on YouTube at https://www.youtube.com/watch?v=s0E1lKHjVv A. This creature has been in fiction, too.

Badger People

Some Indigenous shamans channel their spirits within animals. One of these animals is a badger. Its robust and compact body makes it an excellent and secure form to receive a shapeshifting shaman's spirit. Its black and white stripes suggest a being that stands between night and day, darkness and light.

Indigenous Peoples regard finding badger tracks a sign of good luck. Specifically, the badger's message says we are full of potential and creativity. We just have to activate it!

Indigenous people regard the badger spirit as persistent. Those having trouble tying up loose ends often encounter a badger spirit animal who works on this problem. Badger also comes along to people who don't have much willpower in themselves, offering independence and refreshed resolve.

Lakota tradition regards the badger as an earth animal. Indigenous stories depict the badger as hard-working, protective, and careful. The Pueblo say that the badger is the guardian of the Southern quarter of creation and is associated with the color red. Zunis see the badger as lucky and a healing animal, which is why they often carry stone fetishes of this creature.

Some medicine men believe it is the perfect emissary to meditate the world of spirits and the world of men.

Interestingly, badgers are wild creatures of aggressive behavior. They are dangerous, but they aren't detrimental if you don't annoy them or cause any discomfort. Attempts to handle or trap a badger may cause the animal to bare its teeth or even scratch and bite. Because of a badger's claws and reputation for fearlessness, it is not a good idea to get close to them.

The American badger is a North American badger similar looking to the European badger, although not closely related. This animal lives in the western, central, and eastern United States, northern Mexico, and sections of Canada.

The American badger's habitat includes open grasslands where their available prey live, such as mice, squirrels, and groundhogs. The species prefers areas such as prairie regions with sandy loam soils where it can dig easily for its prey.

Badgers are short-legged omnivores mostly in the family Mustelidae, but also with two species called "badgers" in the related family Mephitidae. While the Mustelidae are a family of carnivorous mammals, including weasels, badgers, otters, ferrets, martens, minks, and wolverines, among others, the Mephitidae is a family of mammals comprising skunks and stink badgers. Badgers are a polyphyletic grouping and are not a natural taxonomic grouping: badgers are united by their squat bodies, adapted for fossorial activity.

There are good reasons a shaman would use the badger as his/her spirit animals to possess. Badgers may appear rather plump, but this is not fat. Rather, it is muscle mass, and the creature is formidable, if need be. Combine this with a powerful jaw, and you have a creature that can stand its ground when necessary. Mind you, the badger would rather find safety than fight, but if they're cornered, they know their assets and use them effectively; this makes this animal a powerful ally when you are developing new attributes and endeavoring to increase self-sufficiency.

Badger is a creature of patience and fortitude. He has a keen mind and prophetic aptitude. This gift from the badger is special because it sees forward while remaining firmly footed in the here-and-now of things. Spiritually, this is a marvelous balance. Other characteristics of the badger spirit include enthusiasm, determination, focus, safety, protection, resolve, strategic planning, and assurance.

I even ran across reports that badgers will sometimes team up with coyotes to hunt. This is a normal behavior in nature. It might be surprising to many people, but it appears coyotes and badgers team up to hunt quite frequently. This partnership is featured in Indigenous storytelling, and even scientists have studied coyote-badger cooperation for quite some time. Something humans can learn to do. On the *Smithsonian Magazine* online, you can view a video showing this. Find it at https://www.smithsonianmag.com/smart-news/watch-coyote-and-badger-hunt-their-prey-together-1-180974170/.

Badgers have often been confused with wolverines in Indigenous folklore—not by the Indigenous People telling the stories, but during their translation into English. While wolverines often are villains or negative characters in Indigenous mythology, the same is not true of badgers, who are usually portrayed as hard-working, cautious animals or as protective parents.

Badgers are also clan animals in some Indigenous cultures. Tribes with Badger Clans include the Hopi (whose Badger Clan is called Honnangyam or Honan-wungwa) and the Pueblo tribes of New Mexico. And not just Indigenous tribes in the Southwest—I found a badger story told by the Lakota Indians (Sioux).

I also discovered that the badger is a shapeshifter in Japanese and Chinese tales.

In Japanese folklore, like the Kitsune (fox) and the tanuki (a Japanese raccoon-dog), mujina (which could be raccoon-dog or badger) are frequently depicted as yōkai that shapeshift and deceive humans. The badger can shapeshift into a man and even sing.

A man sees a badger transforming into a woman playing a shamisen (a stringed instrument) in *Legends of Shimabara.* He believes that the beast is up to no good, so he follows her. As he is about to reveal the woman's identity to his neighbors, the badger drops its illusion. Instead of him staring at a musician, he finds himself looking at a horse's rear end.

Still, this Japanese shifter has been seen in the United States. *Honolulu Advertiser* reporter Bob Krauss reported a mujina at the Waialae Drive-In Theatre in Kahala on May 19, 1959. He noted that a witness watched a woman combing her hair in the women's restroom, and when the witness drew closer, the mujina turned, revealing her featureless face.

The witness later admitted to being admitted to the hospital for a nervous breakdown.

Noted Hawaiian historian, folklorist, and author Glen Grant, in a 1981 radio interview, dismissed the story as a rumor, only to be called by the witness herself, who gave more details on the event, including the previously unreported fact that the mujina in question had red hair. The drive-in no longer exists, having been torn down to make room for Public Storage.

Grant has also reported on several other mujina sightings in Hawaii, from 'Ewa Beach to Hilo.

Though there is nothing about shapeshifting, there is more interesting information about the badger in Celtic beliefs. *Broc* is the word for the badger among the Celts, who respect him for his bravery and unyielding resolve. A Welsh story talks of a badger dream guide to help Pwyll court Rhiannon.

Some parts of Celtic superstition regard the badger as bad luck. Hearing one cry foretells of death or disaster. Having one cross your path isn't good unless they walk across a path you just left.

The Picts held the badger in high regard. So much was the case that their wise men bore the title *Brocan*. The badger's fur was used as an amulet against witchcraft.

Nothing Celtic, but something else concerning the badger: some gambling groups trusted the badger for good fortune at the card table. For this purpose, a gambler might wear a badger's tooth. In folk medicine, the fat of a badger became a rheumatism rub.

The badger shows why of all the shapeshifting creatures, a badger is a good animal to be.

Badger (Public Domain)

How the Dog-Rib Nation Came to Be
Indigenous Myth

An Indigenous tribal legend tells of an Indigenous person who lived along Great Bear Lake. He had a female dog who gave birth to eight puppies. He went out to fish one day and left the puppies tied up in his tent to make sure they wouldn't wander away.

When he returned at the end of the day, he heard children laughing and ran inside the tent, but only found the puppies.

One day, he pretended to leave for a day of fishing, but he hid nearby and waited until he heard the childish laughter and talking, and he busted inside. Eight naked boys and girls were playing. He saw eight skins of puppies nearby, and he snatched them up and tossed them into the fire. From that day on, the children remained human and became the ancestors of the dog-rib nation

.

Conclusion

Dear readers, you reached the last page. I hoped you learned about many of the shapeshifting creatures and those that might have been inspiration for them. There are more on one of those inspirations, the Dogman, but that could be a whole book on its own. So, be sure to google and search for more about them, especially in your own state.

And remember, to make sure the next time you see a crow or a dog in your neighborhood that appears to be staring at you or you heard a growl while you're hitchhiking in the woods, it might be a shapeshifter looking for their next prey. And North America from East Coast to the West Coast, from South all the way up to Alaska, are full of them.

Bibliography

Anne, Christyne; *Nightmare in the Woods*, Self-Published; 2021.

Baker, Linda R.; *American Werewolves (Creatures of the Paranormal)*, Enslow Publishing; 2019.

Bayliss, Clara K; *A Treasury of Eskimo Tales*, Self-Published; 2020.

Blackburn, Lyle; *Sinister Swamps: Monsters and Mysteries from the Mire*, LegendScape Publishing; 2020.

Boyd, Katie; *Werewolves, Myth, Mystery, and Magick*, Schiffer Publishing, LTD, 2011.

Curran, Dr. Bob; Werewolves: *A Field Guide to Shapeshifters, Lycanthropes, and Man-Beasts*, New Page Books; 2009.

Dudding, George; *Dogman: Michigan, Wisconsin, West Virginia*; Self-Published; 2016.

Gerhard, Ken; *A Menagerie of Mysterious Beasts: Encounters with Cryptid Creatures*, Llewellyn Publications; 2016

Gilmore, David D.; *Monsters: Evil Beings, Mythical Beasts, , and All Manner of Imaginary Terrors*, University of Pennsylvania Press; 2009.

Godfrey, Linda S., *American Monsters: A History of Monster Lore, Legends, and Sightings in America*, TarcherPerigee; 2014.

Godfrey, Linda S.; *I Know What I Saw: Modern-Day Encounters with Monsters of New Urban Legend and Ancient Lore*, TarcherPerigee, 2019

Godfrey, Linda S., *Real Wolfmen: True Encounters in Modern America*, TarcherPerigee; 2012.

Guiley, Rosemary Ellen; *Fate Presents Werewolves and Dogmen*, Visionary Living, Inc., 2017.

Guiley, Rosemary Ellen; *Monsters of West Virginia*, Visionary Living, Inc., 2012.

Haggart, GP, *The Michigan Dogman: True Stories from Eyewitnesses*, Self-Published; 2019.

Kinney, Pamela K.; *Haunted Richmond II*, Schiffer Publishing, LTD, 2012.

Kinney, Pamela K.; *Haunted Virginia: Legends, Myths, and True Tales*, Schiffer Publishing, LTD, 2009.

Lyons, Tom; *Dogman Frightening Encounters*, Self-Published;2019.

Mass, Kelly; *Mythology: Aztec, Inca, Inuit, and Polynesian Myths*, Self-Published; 2020

Offutt, Jason, Llewellyn Publications; *Chasing American Monsters: Over 250 Creatures, Cryptids & Hairy Beasts*, Llewellyn Publications; 2019.

Redfern, Nick; *Monster Files, A Look Inside Government Secrets and Classified Documents on Bizarre Creatures and Extraordinary Animals*, Weiser; 2013.

Redfern, Nick; *Shapeshifters: Morphing Monsters & Changing Cryptids*, Llewellyn Publications; 2017.

Redfern, Nick; *The Monster Book: Creatures, Beasts and Fiends of Nature*, Visible Ink Press; 2016.

Baring-Gould, Sabine; *The Book of Werewolves: Being an Account of a Terrible Superstition*, Self-Published; 2016.

Swanson, Gary and Wendy; *The Last Skinwalker: The Avenging Witch of The Navajo Nation*, Self-Published; 2018.

Swanson, Gary and Wendy; *Skinwalkers Shapeshifters and Native American Curses*, Swanson Literary Group, 2017.

Taylor Jr., L. B.; *Monsters of Virginia*, Stackpole Books, 2012.

Weatherly, David; *Monsters of the Last Frontier: Cryptids & Legends of Alaska,* Llewellyn Publications, 2019.

Monsters and Mysteries in America, Season 2, Episode 10, *Travel Channel*

Monsters and Mysteries in America, Season 2, Episode 12, *Travel Channel*

Monsters and Mysteries in America, Season 3, Episode 9, *Travel Channel*

Terror in the Woods, Season 1, Episode 5, *Travel Channel*

The Alaska Triangle, Season 1, Episode 5, *Travel Channel*

Beyond Fringe; The Seven Types of Dogman, *YouTube Channel*

The Mysterious Wolfman of the Great Dismal Swamp, Episode #039, *Encounters with Dogman*, *YouTube Channel*

About the Author

Author Pamela K. Kinney

Author Pamela K. Kinney gave up long ago trying not to listen to the voices in her head and has written award-winning, bestselling horror, fantasy, science fiction, poetry, along with nonfiction ghost books ever since. Three of her nonfiction ghost books garnered Library of Virginia nominations. Her third ghost book, *Virginia's Haunted Historic Triangle: Williamsburg, Yorktown, Jamestown, and Other Haunted Locations*, had reached a second printing and is now a 2nd edition with extra new stories and ten new ghostly images added, plus a new ghost book, *Haunted Surry to Suffolk: Spooky Takes Along Routes 10 and 460* released in 2020 from Anubis Press. Her horror short story, "Bottled Spirits," was runner-up for the 2013 WSFA Small Press Award and is considered one of the seven best genre short fiction for that year. Her latest novel was an urban fantasy, *How the Vortex Changed My Life*. In 2019, her science fiction novella, *Maverick Heart*, released from Dreampunk Press, along with a horror story, "By Midnight," in the Christmas horror and fantasy anthology, *Christmas Lites IX*, and a nonfiction story, "The Haunted Cavalier Hotel," in the paranormal nonfiction anthology, *Handbook for the Dead.* Five micro horror stories of hers in the anthology, Nano *Nightmares,* a horror short story, "Hunting the Goatman," included in the anthology, *Retro Horror,* plus a horror short story, "A Trick, No Treat," and three horror poems of hers, were included in Siren Call Publications' Halloween issue, a poem, "Dementia," in Horror Writers Association's horror poetry anthology, *HWA Poetry Showcase, Vol. VII.* all released in 2020. "Dementia" won "Best Poem" in the poetry category for Critters Readers Poll 2020. She also just had a horror short story, "Family Inheritance," and a poem, "Ghosts," included in the Journal of the Virginia Writers Club, Spring 2021, and a horror short story, "Death of the Apostrophe," in the spring issue of Siren Call Publications. In 2022, she will have a Halloween horror story, "Pumpkin Hollow," included in the *Horror for Halloween* anthology to be published by Dreampunk Press.

Pamela and her husband live with one crazy black cat (who thinks she should take precedence over her mistress's writing most days). Along with writing, Pamela has acted on stage and film and investigates the paranormal for episodes of Paranormal World Seekers for AVA Productions. She is a member of both Horror Writers Association and Virginia Writers Club. You can learn more about Pamela K. Kinney at http://www.PamelaKKinney.com.

CPSIA information can be obtained
at www.ICGtesting.com
Printed in the USA
BVHW031135070822
644000BV00003B/7